FUNdamental Soccer

Written by **Karl Dewazien**
United States Soccer Federation "A" Licensed Coach

*I will use "HE", in this book, generically to refer to both
boys and girls for the sake of brevity.*

Karl Dewazien

c 1992, by **Karl Dewazien**

ISBN 0-9619139-3-2

Printed by **Pyramid Printing**   Fresno, California

Book design and illustrations **Joseph G. Garcia**

Editors: **Terri Monson**
          Vincent J. Lavery

FUN Soccer Enterprises
2904 Fine Ave.
Clovis, CA. 93612

D0107806

1

INTRODUCTION

Soccer is a simple game to understand...it is a contest between two teams of equal numbers. Once a team has control of the ball...**all** the players become part of the **Attacking team**...and their aim is to control, pass, dribble and shoot the ball across the opponents goal line, underneath the crossbar and between the goal posts for a score. Should the team lose possession of the ball, an immediate transition takes place, and **all** players become part of the **Defending team**...and their aim is to make every effort to regain ball possession and prevent the opponent from scoring. The main objective of the game is to **score more goals than your opponent.**

Soccer is a simple game to play...requiring simple skills (control, dribble, pass and shooting the ball)... and what makes great soccer players is **perfecting these simple skills.**

Soccer is a simple game to coach...requiring simple skills (read, study and understand the information presented in the "FUNdamental SOCCER" book & video series)... and what will make you a successful youth soccer coach is the **application of this information.**

TABLE OF CONTENTS

Section 1. KNOW...YOUR PLAYERS ———————— Page 4

...EIGHT STEPS OF LEARNING ———————— Page 8

...TEN STEPS OF TEACHING ———————— Page 10

Section 2. PLANNING CONSIDERATIONS ———————— Page 19

Section 3. ORGANIZING THE PRACTICE ———————— Page 29
(In Eight Steps)

Section 4. DRIBBLING ———————— Page 46

Section 5. USING THE INSTEP FOR SHOOTING ———————— Page 72

Section 6. GROUND PASSING ———————— Page 94

Section 7. WALL PASS ———————— Page 110

Section 8. CONTROLLING GROUND BALL ———————— Page 114

Section 9. CONTROLLING FLIGHTED BALL ———————— Page 116

Section 10. THROW-IN ———————— Page 118

Section 11. SMALL SIDED GAMES ———————— Page 120

GET TO KNOW YOUR PLAYERS.

Make a conscientious effort to *get to know each player on a personal basis*.

Talk about mutual goals both short and long term.

Make all conversation "two-way".

During these talks it is *very important* to find out...
If the player is really interested in playing soccer?

NOTE: It is an irrefutable fact that *all young players are beginners and learners* and that *older players* may be more advanced but they *also need to learn more.*

GENERALLY SPEAKING:

The decision to play soccer in the U-10 age group is influenced by ***Parents**	The decision to play soccer in the U-14 age group is influenced by ***Peers**

In both instances you will be faced with *players who are not interested in playing soccer* and adjustments must be made accordingly...

Give appropriate attention to the disinterested player but not at the expense of the rest of the team.

Make the practices so much FUN that the disinterested player will want to join!

NOTES FOR BETTER COACHING

1. Be patient!

2. Try to improve **one** technique at each practice session.

3. Prepare them for the unexpected in the game.

4. Provide only **one** tip/suggestions on improvement at a time.

5. Permit the players to make mistakes and learn from their mistakes.

6. Encourage the player when appropriate.

7. Focus on individual improvement rather than comparing with others.

5. Encourage questions and discussions.

9. Urge the players to practice their technique for short periods each day (homework).

10. They will continue to participate if they are having FUN.

REMEMBER, EVERYTHING TAKES TIME TO LEARN.

OBSERVING

By **watching** the coach, advanced players, videos or film on the technique they are to perform.

FEELING

By **touching** the part of the foot or body which will be involved when they perform the technique.

HEARING

By **listening** "carefully" to instructions when they are given.

VISUALIZING

By **seeing themselves** performing the technique.

IMITATING
By **re-enacting** the technique observed.

SELF-TALKING
By **repeating the "buzz words"** while they are imitating.

PRACTICING
By **repeating the proper use of the technique**... correcting mistakes in the process...until its perfected and **becomes a Habit.**

TESTING
By **playing against others,** checking progress...first, in practice then in an actual game.

KNOW HOW TO TEACH

Step 1. EXPLANATION. (Coach)

Communicate in simple everyday language.

Create or use "buzz words" (Words that "trigger" the mind to highlighted points of emphasis)

FOR EXAMPLE

Controlling the ball...
"Behind...Relax...Re-direct"

Dribbling..."*Push...stop...step*"

Passing..."*Plant...Lock... Follow through*"

Shooting..."*Push...glance...place*"

Helpful Hints:

Take into consideration the *attention span* of your players and *adjust* the length of your explanation *accordingly*.................**Be brief!**

After you have dealt with a point...*ask questions* to make sure the point was understood; *repeat* the verbal instructions *only if necessary* ....**Be brief!**

I HEAR AND I FORGET ....**Be brief!**

10

Step 2. DEMONSTRATION. (Coach)

Give a **demonstration**-slowly---simply----and technically correct.

Make it completely clear what points the demonstration is intended to bring out.

IMPORTANT:

If you are unable to demonstrate, then have *a guest instructor* or one of your *better players* do the demonstration for you!.

While the demonstration is taking place make sure that everything can be seen clearly by all players.

I SEE AND I REMEMBER.... **...........Slow, correct and brief!**

11

Step 3. TOUCHING. (Players)

As the demonstration and explanation are taking place...

Have the players make contact with **(touch)** the part of the shoe or body which will come into play when they perform the technique.

IMPORTANT:
This helps in programming the brain and muscles to work together.

Step 4. VISUALIZING. (Players)

After the demonstration/explanation and touching...

Have the players close their eyes and **imagine** themselves *performing the technique* correctly and proficiently...

IMPORTANT:
This powerful method is currently being used by many international athletes who realize that *the body can better achieve what the mind has rehearsed.*

Step 5. **SELF-TALK.** (Players)
As they are "visualizing"...

Have the players repeat the "buzz words"...**out-loud!**

PUSH! STOP! STEP! PLANT! LOCK! PLACE!

This will let you know if:
They listened to your instructions.
They are indeed ...visualizing...or just resting their eyes.

Step 6. **INVOLVEMENT..** (Players)
After using the previously mentioned confidence building tools ...

Divide the team into working units.

INDIVIDUAL — GROUP — TEAM

TAKE INTO CONSIDERATION:

Who will be partners. Match basic skill level.	*Distance from the partners.* From close work to distance they can effectively handle.
Area of performance. Primary zone of players responsibility.	*Number of opponents.* Guarantee success!

I DO AND I UNDERSTAND.......
Activity, good repetition, experimentation and enjoyment--lead to success!

Step 7. **OBSERVE.** (Coach)

As the players experiment with performing the technique...

Look for weaknesses in the execution of the movement/technique.

VERY IMPORTANT:

Discipline your mind to focus only on what is being taught...
and *ignoring all other mistakes*.

AVOID CAUSING PARALYSIS THROUGH ANALYSIS

Step 8. **CORRECT**. (Coach)

Consistent basic faults can be corrected by:

Asking guided questions.

Using the "sandwich approach"
Begin with **a positive statement**...
follow with **the constructive criticism**...
and end with **a positive statement!**

Reverse coaching---Have the player teach you!

Repetition of movement---Have the player do the action very slowly!

Kinesiology--Physically adjust the player's body to help him achieve the correct form through a realization of how it "feels".

Helpful Hints:

Learning takes place, *resulting from errors made*, if the player is instructed correctly both verbally and physically.

When in doubt, **GO BACK TO BASICS**
...break down the skill to its component parts.

VERY IMPORTANT:
IN *ALL* CASES RESTART ACTION WITH CORRECT MOVE OR MANEUVER.

Step 9. **TEST.** (Players)

*Perform the technique against **one** opponent.*

Opponent increases defensive pressure as confidence and ability increase:

Begin with a *walking* opponent.	Advance to a *jogging* opponent.	Finally... the opponent plays at *game speed*!

Helpful Hint:
Be careful that in the haste of competing
the technique does not deteriorate.

Step 10. **CONFIRM.** (Coach)

Critique to see what learning has taken place!

Helpful Hint:
Do not expect to see in a game anything that was not accomplished in practice.

THROUGHOUT THIS *TEN STEP TEACHING* SEQUENCE...

BE PATIENT...You must not expect immediate results

BE PERSISTENT...It will take time and effective repetition.

BE FLEXIBLE...So that you can maintain players' interest when working on a particular soccer technique.

MAINTAIN THAT SENSE OF HUMOR... The players should work in a relaxed atmosphere.

REWARD...with a positive *reaction*, a positive *comment* or just a *smile*.

REMEMBER, EVERYTHING TAKES TIME TO LEARN!!!

AN INARGUABLE FACT:

Your players will progress through their motor development sequence at their own pace.

REMEMBER, they had to crawl, walk, run, jump, hop, in that order, so they will develop their soccer skills the same way...

oooooooooooooooooooooooooooooooooooooooooooooooooooo

BALL CONTROL - DRIBBLING - SHOOTING - PASSING

The important thing is that a child shows continued progress.

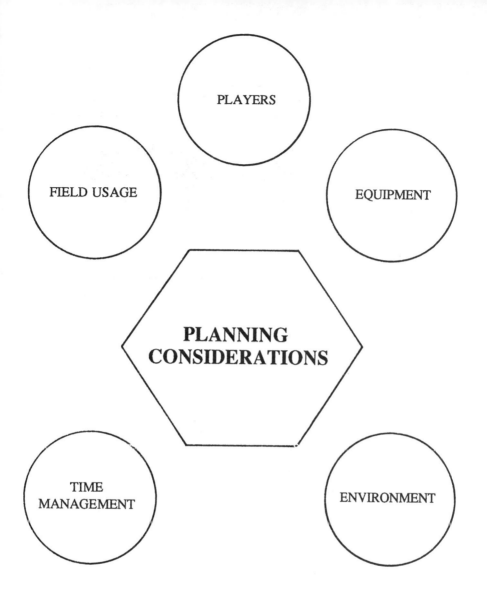

PLAYERS

FIELD USAGE

EQUIPMENT

PLANNING CONSIDERATIONS

TIME MANAGEMENT

ENVIRONMENT

Prior Planning Prevents Poor Practices!

PLAYERS

TO FUNCTION AS:

TEAMMATES For Realism Establish Familiarity	OPPONENTS For Realism Force Decision Making
Number at practice	**Age**
Interests CONSIDER	**Needs**

TECHNICALLY

WEAK	STRONG
work with the ball	work with and without the ball
LARGE FIELD OF PLAY	SMALL FIELD OF PLAY
less opposing players	more opposing players

Work with the ball--
  TO *develop* soccer *technique and* build ball control *confidence.*

Large field of play--
  TO keep the ball in *continuous play.*
  TO provide *more space* in which to perform .
  TO create more opportunities to *recover after making a mistake.*

Fewer opposing players--
  TO *assure* an increased number of *touches with the ball.*
  TO create more opportunities to *succeed against opposition.*

As players become *more proficient* in using the basic techniques of the game *against opposition*...PLAN AND ACT ACCORDINGLY!

FIELD USAGE

FIELDS WITHIN THE FIELD
Sectionalizing the field to achieve maximum learning.

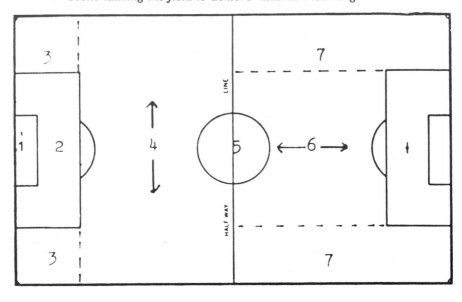

COACHING GRIDS

CHECKERBOARD SYSTEM

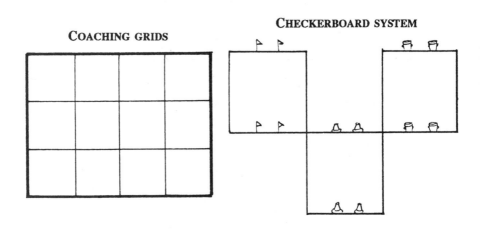

NOTE:

Your *use of cones, flags and other markers becomes extremely important* **if you do not have** the luxury of being able to use **marked fields.**

GOALS...

VITAL: All practice games must include two Targets...

| **ONE to *ATTACK*** | **ONE to *DEFEND*** |

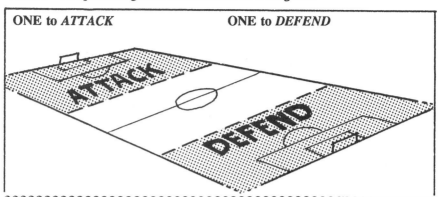

Players must instinctively respond by ***READING ball possession.***
This means...

| **OUR** ball = "*READ*" = ATTACK | **THEIR** ball = "*READ*" = DEFEND |

Two dimensional players (*ones who can Attack & Defend*) are developed in this *habit forming environment.*

| **Bad habits** are created in *BAD practices.* | **Good habits** are created in *GOOD practices.* |

NOTE:

> Your *use of cones, flags and other markers becomes extremely important* **if you do not have** the luxury of being able to use **regulation soccer goals.**

EQUIPMENT
COACH'S RESPONSIBILITY (Team manager)

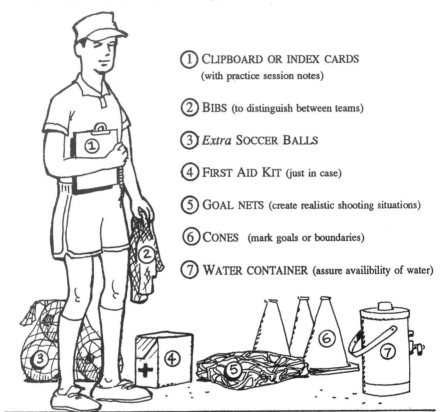

1. CLIPBOARD OR INDEX CARDS (with practice session notes)

2. BIBS (to distinguish between teams)

3. *Extra* SOCCER BALLS

4. FIRST AID KIT (just in case)

5. GOAL NETS (create realistic shooting situations)

6. CONES (mark goals or boundaries)

7. WATER CONTAINER (assure availibility of water)

OPTIONAL ITEMS:

Air pump & needle (properly inflate balls)

Whistle (game control and assembly)

Pen and Note pad (jot down important notes for future review)

Watch (stop and start on time)

Stopwatch (to time improvement & events)

Marking pen (for identification marking player/team articles)

Magnetic playing field (to use as visual aid)

Tape recorder (music for warm-up and crowd noise during practice)

24

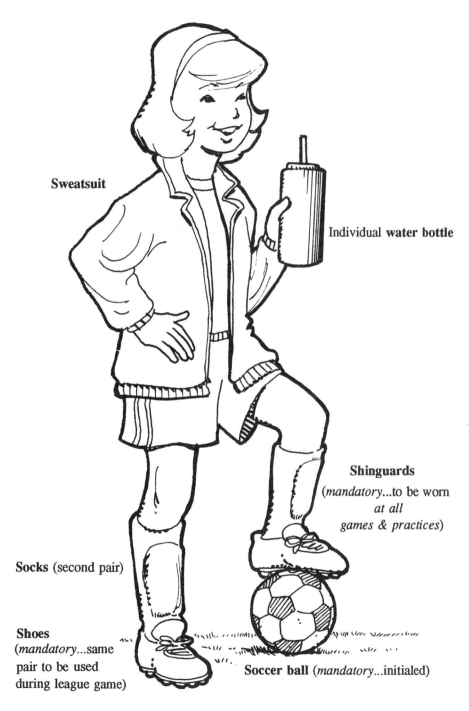

Sweatsuit

Individual **water bottle**

Shinguards
(*mandatory*...to be worn
at all
games & practices)

Socks (second pair)

Shoes
(*mandatory*...same
pair to be used
during league game)

Soccer ball (*mandatory*...initialed)

TIME MANAGEMENT

Evaluate how well time is being used.

MINIMIZE LISTENING AND LECTURE TIME.

MAXIMIZE TOUCHES WITH THE BALL AND PLAYING TIME.

IDEALLY, Length of practice should be:

PREPARATION....................................*10 MINUTES*

ACTIVITY...(Playing/Teaching)........*Length of League Game*

4 vs.1

OBSERVE & HELP

4 vs.3

4 vs.2

CLOSING ....*10 MINUTES*

Example:
Preparation = 10 minutes   League game = 40 minutes   Closing = 10 minutes

Length of practice = 60 minutes

ENVIRONMENT

The genius of good coaching is to make hard work seem like FUN.

Ask yourself-DOES IT HAPPEN IN THE GAME?
*If the answer is **NO***, THEN DO NOT PRACTICE IT!

For example: **STANDING IN LINES.**

VERY IMPORTANT:
Duplicate the excitement of the game in your practice sessions!

Create an atmosphere where the players are allowed to teach themselves.

IF PRACTICE IS:

Too *simple*...They will get *bored*.

Too *complex*...They will get *confused*.

Be *CREATIVE*...So that *learning* will continuously take place.

Helpful Hints:
Consider the present skill level of each player then gear exercises and games so the player is challenged.
Create an environment which forces the players to make decisions and learn on their own.

ORGANIZING THE PRACTICE

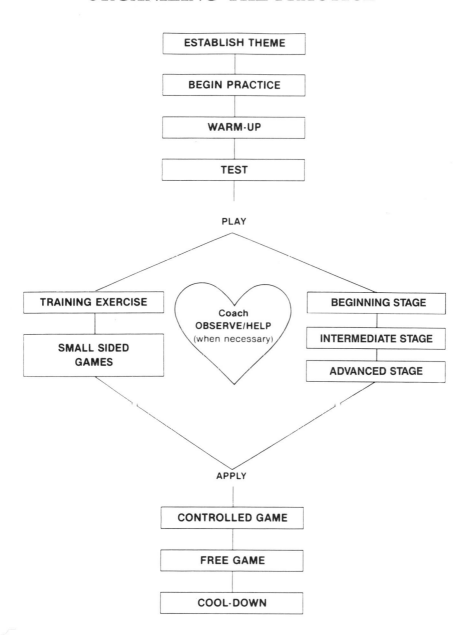

ESTABLISH THEME

BEGIN PRACTICE

WARM-UP

TEST

PLAY

TRAINING EXERCISE

Coach
OBSERVE/HELP
(when necessary)

BEGINNING STAGE

SMALL SIDED
GAMES

INTERMEDIATE STAGE

ADVANCED STAGE

APPLY

CONTROLLED GAME

FREE GAME

COOL-DOWN

ORGANIZING THE PRACTICE

Step 1. ESTABLISH THE THEME.

*Carefully **observe** your team in action and **determine:***

Who is having problems?

What is the **major** problem/weakness?

KEY on this *ONE topic ...THE THEME.*
To be discussed, developed and improved at the next practice session.

Helpful Hints:

Take mental and written *notes.*

*Great observers **avoid** being ball watchers; becoming emotionally involved in the action; managing players' actions; assessing and assisting the referee!*

ORGANIZING THE PRACTICE

Step 2. **BEGIN THE PRACTICE SESSION.**

Gather--Bring the players to a *defined comfortable area.*

Socialize--Allow each player to *say something*!

Name the THEME--
Tell the players what they are expected *to learn or improve.*
State *clearly* the **ONE** goal to be achieved!

Teach the THEME
Coach--player-or-guest...

Give a *concise*
EXPLANATION/DEMONSTRATION
of the **THEME.**

Players... **Observe,** | **Listen** | and **Touch.**

Step 3. **WARM UP...and** (Review)

A. **Pre-Stretch...**(Play a FUN-game)

Preparing players for the rigorous activity of a practice or game *is vitally important.* Most fitness experts agree that a *warm up* is essential *for optimal performance* and *injury prevention.* The initial stage should consist of **light running** or **jogging** to increase the blood supply to the muscles, increase the rate and force of muscle contractions and raise the body and muscle temperature.

How can you tell when the players are ready to stretch?

They should be slightly out of breath and should have broken "the sweat barrier."

Running laps may be considered as *punishment.*

FUN game...Disguise the fact that they are working hard.

B. Stretch.

For the prevention of injuries, a coach must understand that a player's muscles are surrounded by a sheath of connective tissue called the epimysium. Unless the epimysium is allowed to expand, the muscles will be restricted from a full range of motion, and maximum work capacity from these hindered muscles cannot be expected. *Forcing a player to jerk, jump, or run into a state of feeling loose can be harmful,* for this procedure may put a hole in the epimysium resulting in a sprain, internal bleeding, or other related muscle injuries. The introduction of a *slow deliberate "eight-count" stretching routine* is a means toward solving muscle injury problems. The "eight-count" stretching exercises are held to the point where tension is felt and then followed by a brief moment of relaxation. All subsequent movements stretch the muscle group beyond the initial point and continue until the muscle is allowed to *stretch to its fullest range of motion.* Each exercise is performed for at least *one minute per muscle group.* But, an entire *stretching routine need not last longer than ten minutes* to be effective.

Ruling principle = Slow and Easy!

C. Ball gymnastics...

Personal challenge and FUN. Feeling for movement and coordination of/with the ball.

D. Review...

THE WARM-UP PERIOD SHOULD ALSO BE USED FOR A **REVIEW** OF **TECHNIQUES** TAUGHT IN PREVIOUS SESSIONS... **TO** PROVIDE CONTINUITY.

ORGANIZING THE PRACTICE
Step 4. **TESTING.**

Purpose: To convince the player of his need to practice the weakness that YOU observed during the last game.

Note: YOU must *recreate the exact conditions under which the player failed* to carry out the needed skill.

EXAMPLE: ⬤⬤⬤⬤⬤⬤⬤⬤⬤⬤⬤⬤⬤⬤⬤⬤⬤⬤⬤⬤⬤

Your **OBSERVATION: Major weakness** was accuracy in *passing over the shorter distances* (5-10 yards).

Your **THEME: Improve short passing** accuracy on the ground.

Suggested **TEST:** Each player to be given 10 attempts.

PLAYERS GRID	DISTANCE GRID (5-10 YDS)	DISTANCE GRID (5-10 YDS)	PLAYERS GRID

Score card: Out of 10 Attempts

SCORE	CONCLUSION	NEED	ACTION
1-3	very poor	Demo/Explain/Practice	FUNdamental Stage
4-5	weak	Demo/Practice	Game related Stage
6-7	good	Practice	Game condition Stage
8-10	excellent	Play	Small sided game *Special rules— –teams must be uneven –two touch play –passes must be on the ground

---

NOTE: *Avoid comparisons with others.* Encourage each player to concentrate on self-improvement rather than on keeping up with others.

ORGANIZING THE PRACTICE

BEFORE proceeding to Step 5...(*if necessary*)

QUICKLY **repeat the demonstration** and
use only the "buzz" words introduced earlier.

TOUCH   STOP   STEP   CHANGE DIRECTION

THEN have the players... VISUALIZE... VERBALIZE...and DO IT!

STOP   STEP
TOUCH   CHANGE DIRECTIONS

TOUCH   STOP   STEP   CHANGE DIRECTIONS

Step 5. PLAY... (OBSERVE & HELP!)

SMALL SIDED GAMES (Related to the Theme):

Games framed inside a set of rules to correct faults observed in the last game.

EXAMPLE: 4 vs. 2

BENEFIT OF THESE GAMES:

Creates an atmosphere where **technique can be observed under game related conditions.**

- Fulfills the **main objective** of any practice session **--maximum touches of the ball** in minimum amount of time.

  - **Involves maximum number of players** in a minimum amount of space.

    - Creates **competitive atmosphere** resulting in improving physical fitness, technique and variety **to keep players interested.**

MOST IMPORTANT:

Allows the coach opportunities to
...TEACH WITHOUT DISRUPTING OTHERS.

4 vs. 3

4 vs. 1

OBSERVE & HELP

4 vs. 2

SEE SMALL SIDED GAME SECTION (PAGE 120) FOR DETAILED RULES

PLAY... (OBSERVE & HELP!)
STAGES of PROGRESSION

A. BEGINNING STAGE
Performed with pressure of **imaginary OR walking opponent(s).**

The players perform the technique **technically correct** at a slow pace
...while **saying the "buzz" words...**

Increasing the speed of movement and *eliminating the "buzz" words*
is part of the progression as the players become more proficient.

Helpful Hints... Create an **atmosphere:**
Where player(s) can **experiment** with their **strengths** and **weaknesses.**
At a **distance** from partner(s) where performance will be **successful.**
At a **speed** where movement and action is **slower** to allow learning
to take place.
With **ample time** to **concentrate** on perfect execution.

PLAY... (OBSERVE & HELP!)
STAGES of PROGRESSION

B. INTERMEDIATE STAGE

Performed with pressure of **imaginary OR jogging opponent(s).**

OR   **Versus time...** (the clock)

Helpful Hints... Create an **atmosphere:**

Where player(s) **are challenged** to deal with their strength and weakness.

At a **distance** from partner(s) where there is **probability of success.**

At a faster **speed...**(As close to game condition as possible)

With **restricted time** to challenge the player.

PLAY... (OBSERVE & HELP!)
STAGES of PROGRESSION

C. ADVANCED STAGE

Performed with pressure of **active opponents...at game speed!**

Where players are **constantly challenged** by an opponent. 	At **distance** from partner(s) as **in** an actual **game.** 
Where **speed** of movement is **dictated by** the pressure of the **opponent.** 	With **time** that would be given **in** an actual **game.** 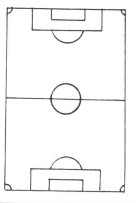

Helpful Hints:

Be careful that in the haste of competing -**technique does not deteriorate.**
Recognize fatigue and when it becomes factor in learning.
Include active/inactive rest periods when the activity is at a high pace.

When in doubt...**GO BACK TO BASICS**...slow down the action

ORGANIZING THE PRACTICE

Step 6. PLAY A CONTROLLED GAME (Ruled by the coach)
Alter the scrimmage in such a way that a particular technique or tactic is emphasized.

Examples:

1. GHOST SOCCER
  a. Team **vs. no one** (Shadow training)--Coach specifies pass & running routes

  b. Team **vs. time**   (against stop watch)

2. THINKING - OUT - LOUD SOCCER
  Coach calls out passes, shots, running routes etc..

Good -If infrequent calls by someone who knows the game. (not idle chatter)
Bad -If used too often, players will not learn to think for themselves

CONTROLLED GAMES (continued)

3. FREEZE GAME

On a pre-arranged signal everyone stops.

To...

..rectify faults immediately, instant feedback.
..avoid possible mistake coming up.
..avoid the situation to change drastically.
..allow the players to recall the situation.

4. DEAD BALL SITUATION - COACHING

Coach recreates the situation when the ball is not in play.
Make sure you observed what you will talk about.
Be specific ... *do not ramble.*
Tailor your talk to the age group you are working with, *be simple.*

Helpful Hints:

Do not be sidetracked by other mistakes...*stick to your Theme.*
Do not abuse these games...*create a flow in the action.*

VERY IMPORTANT:
IN *ALL* CASES RESTART ACTION WITH CORRECT MOVE OR MANEUVER.

Step 7. **PLAY A FREE GAME** (Controlled by the players)

Discipline yourself to know when to leave the players alone!

REMEMBER: Over coaching can often be worse than no coaching!

Step 8. **COOL-DOWN**

Many coaches fail to remember the tremendous physical/mental punishment their players must endure during practice and game situations. The **cool-down** period **must become an integral part of every coaches training/playing routine.**

A. PHYSICAL COOL-DOWN

The PHYSICAL goal is to relieve the tightness created by running and other soccer related activities. Stress on the lower back is compounded by the unnatural kicking movements and jarring effects from landing on the solid surface of the playing field resulting in a narrowing of the spinal vertebrae. *Stretching the spine and opening the narrowed spaces are necessary. A slow jog and some stretching exercises are sufficient for this training phase.*

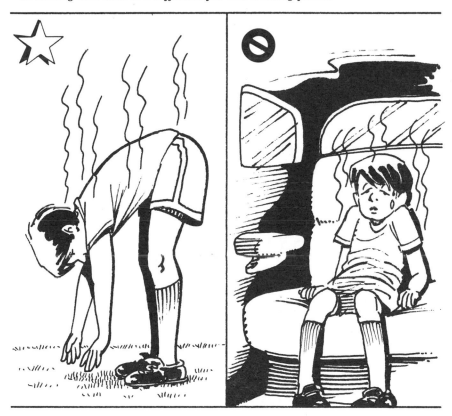

IMPORTANT:
1. **To prevent soreness and injury...***Stretches should be done after every practice and game.*
2. **If you are going to stretch only once,** *AFTERWARDS, is the most important time.*

43

B. MENTAL COOL-DOWN.

The MENTAL goal is to relieve the tension created by spectators, peers or personal mistakes. *After a practice* the player *must feel prepared for the next game. After a loss* a feeling of accomplishment, not failure, must be created. And *after a win*, players must be made aware that more improvement can take place.

Briefly analyze the strong and weak points of their performance.

IMPORTANT:
1. Encouragement helps to **increase natural enthusiasm.**
2. Coaches must **encourage effort, not results.**

44

PRACTICE SESSION
(EXAMPLE)

Date: Location: Starting Time:
                                                 Ending Time:

A. OBSERVATION:
Major weakness ability to maintain ball possession in 1 vs 1 situations.

B. THEME: *Dribbling*

C. WARM-UP:
　　　　　Fun game: *Confined area game... "Bumper cars"*
　　　　　Stretching: *Two players... One ball routine*

D. TEST: *Not necessary...last game showed obvious weakness.*

E. WHILE PLAYERS ARE PLAYING IN SMALL SIDED GAMES:
All games will be even sided....(1 vs 1) but no more than (3 vs 3)

Observe for weaknesses in dribbling move being taught.
Help only those who are in need of assistance by taking
them out of the games and through the **stages of progression.**
　　　Reminder...
　　　Beginning Stage: *imaginary or walking opponent.*
　　　Intermediate Stage: *imaginary or jogging opponent.*
　　　Advanced Stage: *active opponent...at game speed.*

F. CONTROLLED GAME: *(Five vs Five)*

Rule: *Each player must touch the ball (10) times...
before they can pass to a teammate.*

G. FREE GAME: *Split team in half...play across half field.*

H. COOL-DOWN:
　　　　　Physical...*normal stretching routine.*
　　　　　Mental...*positive comments and talk about upcoming opponent.*

THEME: DRIBBLING

Just as a child cannot run until he has mastered crawling and walking, the player cannot train or play effectively until he has mastered dribbling.

Dribbling, as defined in this book, is the art of maneuvering the ball with the feet in order to maintain ball possession. Much of the skill amounts to the ability to control the ball while running, stopping and turning at various speeds. Deceptive body movements in combination with foot maneuvers are used to beat the opponent.

THE MASTERING OF DRIBBLING SHOULD BE ACCOMPLISHED BEFORE EMPHASIZING OTHER TECHNIQUES.
An effective dribbler can:

- Keep the ball until a teammate is in a clear position to receive a pass.
- Get past a defender thus gaining numerical superiority on the attack.
- Clear oneself for a shot on goal.

KEY POINTS:

1. The upper body should be tilted slightly forward — to further screen the ball.

2. The ball should be played (touched) on the side of the toe using either the inside or outside of the foot.

LEFT SHOE		RIGHT SHOE	
OUTSIDE INSTEP	INSIDE INSTEP	INSIDE INSTEP	OUTSIDE INSTEP

3. The eyes should be fixed partially on the ball — in addition to peripherally encompassing "the action around the player".

VISION

VISION

YES

VISION

NO   NO

46

WARM-UP (Before stretching)

The purpose of this segment is to:
- Prepare the body for stretching.
- Begin working on one's dribbling techniques.
- Have some FUN.

FUNgames

"SIMON SAYS"

Objective: Follow instructions after hearing "SIMON SAYS".

Rules:
- Coach calls out "SIMON SAYS" and instruction.
- Player not following instruction by "SIMON SAYS" is eliminated. (#)

Winner: Last player in the game.

CRAB MONSTERS

Objective: Dribblers maintain ball possession against "Crab" players.

Rules:
- Dribbler attempts to move to end of channel.
- "Crab" attempts to rob dribbler by kicking ball out of channel.
- Player who loses ball becomes an additional "Crab".

Winner: Last Dribbler in the game.

VARIATION: May be played as a team game.

(#) Keep eliminated player active by working with the ball away from the contest.

47

DRIBBLING (Warm-Up)
FUNgames
FOLLOW THE LEADER

Number of Players:	Partners.
Equipment:	Each player with a ball.
Objective:	Mirror partners' moves.
Rules:	Imitate partners' moves.

VARIATION: Have the full team follow ONE leader.

CHAIN GANG

Number of players:	Three or more players linked by one hand on partners' shoulder.
Equipment:	One ball per linked group—"chain".
Objective:	Dribbling the ball without breaking the link.
Rule:	• Once link is broken, go back to start.
Winners:	First "chain" to go through an obstacle course. First "chain" to go across a finish line.

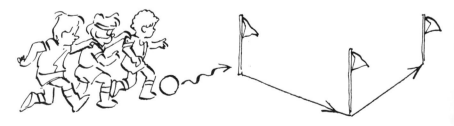

VARIATION: Soccer game of "chains" playing each other.

FUNgames

CONFINED AREA GAMES

These guidelines and rules apply to the following games:

1. Number of Players: Full team.
2. Equipment: One ball per player.
3. Playing area marked out — size depends on age, skill level and number of players involved.
4. Have a stated playing time for each contest.
5. Each contest should start with a "signal".
6. Players must stay in constant motion dribbling the ball.
7. Losing possession of one's ball or moving outside of defined area results in elimination or a point against.

BUMPER CARS

Objective: Avoid hitting other players with body or touching their ball.

Rules: • Hitting other players or touching their ball results in a citation.
Five citations and player goes to jail.

Winner: Player with the least citations at end of regulation time.

KING OF DRIBBLERS

Objective: Maintain ball possession.

Rule: • Each player protects his own ball and attempts to kick any other player's ball out of the confined area.

Winner: Last player in ball possession.

VARIATION: Divide the team in half.
Winners: Team with most players left at the time limit.

49

FUNgames

JAWS

Objective: Maintain ball possession.

Rules: • One player is designated as "JAWS". "JAWS" enters the field of play and attempts to kick other players' balls out.

Winner: Last player in possession of ball.

VARIATION: More than one player designated as "JAWS".

MUSICAL SOCCER BALL.

Objective: Place ball at feet at signal.

Rules: • One player starts the contest without a ball.
• On a signal the player enters the field of play and gets a ball.
• Players who lost a ball must try to get yet another ball.
• Player may not try for the ball he has lost — must try for someone elses.

Winners: Players with ball at the conclusion of the contest.

VARIATION: Begin the contest with more than one player without the ball.

FUNgames

WHERE AM I GOING?

Objective: All players try to touch "numbered marker" as indicated by coach.

Field of play: Each corner must be numbered — one through four.

Rules:
- Player moves to "numbered corner" as directed by the coach.
- Player may not play opponent's ball. (Variation: Player may play opponent's ball.)

Winners: All players except last one to touch marker with the ball.

VARIATION: Team game — divide team in half — last one on team to touch that team loses.

MASS MIGRATION

Objective: To get your group into the second grid before the opponent does — with ball under control.

Field of play: Two outlined areas — minimum 10 yards apart.

Number of Players: Two teams — any number of players.

Rules:
- Coach gives specific instructions inside first area. (Ex: dribble in circles — right foot only.)
- Player may not play opponent's ball — offending player will be last allowed out of the first grid.
- On signal — all players run and dribble to the second grid.

Winners: First team to get all players into second grid with ball under control.

VARIATION: Players may play opponent's ball.

FUNgames

TRAFFIC EXCHANGE

Objective:	To get your group into the second grid before the opponent does with ball under control.
Field of play:	Two outlined areas — minimum 10 yards apart.
Number of Players:	Two teams — any number of players.
Rules:	• Coach gives specific instructions inside first area.
	• On signal all players run and dribble their ball to the second grid.
	• Players may not touch each other or the ball when the exchange is taking place — offending players go back to starting grid to run again.
Winners:	First group to get all players into second grid with ball under control.

GREEN!

VARIATION: Players may play opponent's ball during the exchange.

52

FUNgames

WHERE ARE WE GOING?

Objective:
To get group into "called grid" before the opponent — with ball under control.

Field of play:
Three outlined areas — minimum of 10 yards apart.

Number of Players:
Two teams — any number of players.

Rules:
- Coach gives specific instructions for inside center grid.
- Players may not touch each other or the ball when inside the center grid — offending players are last to be allowed out of the center grid.
- Coach calls out "left" or "right".

Winners:
First group to get into the "called grid" with ball under control.

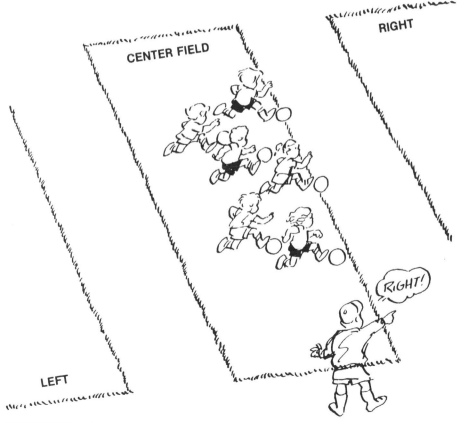

VARIATION: Players are allowed to interfere with the opponent at any time.

FUNgames

MARTIAN INVADERS (SINGLE)

Equipment:	Twelve soccer balls placed in center of grid.
Objective:	To be the first to get 4 balls to their corner.
Number of Players:	Four players per grid — start with one on each corner.
Rules:	• On signal, players run to retrieve balls for their corner.
	• Once no balls are left in the center, players may rob each other.
Winner:	First to get 4 balls to his corner.

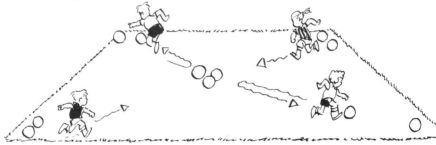

MARTIAN INVADERS (GROUP)

Equipment:	Twelve soccer balls.
Objective:	To be the first group to get 4 balls to their corner.
Number of Players:	Team divided into four groups of three.
Rules:	• On signal, players run to other groups to steal balls.
	• Players may not protect their corner.
	• No passing is allowed.
	• No interfering with other players' dribble.
Winners:	First group with four balls in their corner.

VARIATION: Allow interference with other groups dribbling from start of contest.

FUNgames

CAT & MOUSE (SINGLES)

Objective:	Maintain ball possession within grid boundaries.
Number of Players:	One versus One.
Rules:	• When ball goes over boundaries other player brings it back into play with opponent four yards away.
	• Vary the number of contests according to the physical conditioning of your players.
Winner:	Player who has ball possession at one minute time limit.

CAT & MOUSE (GROUP GAME)

Equipment:	All players have a ball — except "CAT".
Objective:	Be the last player to get caught.
Number of Players:	Full team.
Rules:	• "CAT" calls for "MICE" to run from North to South or East to West to across safe line. When player is robbed of ball, that player also becomes a "CAT".
Winner:	Last mouse to have ball possession.

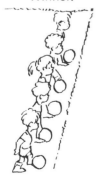  

VARIATION: "CAT" can call ONE player at a time from starting line.

DAILY ROUTINE

Objectives: To develop ball sensitivity, co-ordination, flexibility, agility, body control — in short, confidence in keeping possession of the ball.

DANCING STORK

Stationary ball.
Place right sole on the ball — then hop on left foot with right returning to ball. (Switch feet)

Move ball
While hopping on right foot, move the ball right, left, forward and backward using the sole of left foot.

VARIATION: "Ball contact Foot" touches with outer-inner instep.

KANGAROO DANCE

Stationary ball.
While hopping, alternate foot touches (sole) with the top of the ball.

Move ball.
While hopping, move the ball right, left, forward and backward while alternating right and left foot touches (sole).

SOCCER BOXING

In one spot — While dancing tap the ball from the inside of other foot.

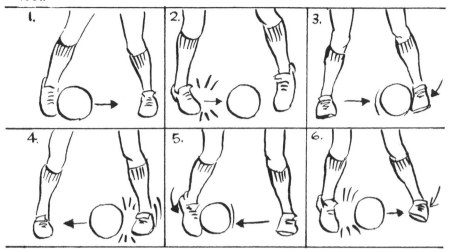

Moving around — While dancing tap the ball from inside and move left, right, backward and forward.

SOCCER BOXING (Variation)

In one spot — While dancing tap the ball from the inside of one foot to the instep of other foot. (NOTE: Turn instep towards ball).

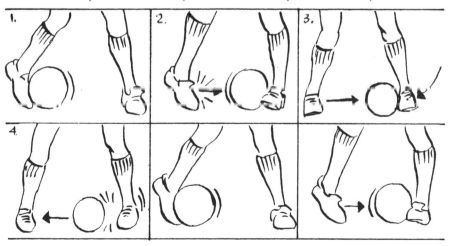

Moving around — While dancing tap the ball from inside to instep and move left, right, backward and forward.

MORE: The ball can also be tapped from one instep to the other while applying the above instructions.

REMEMBER THE STAGES OF PROGRESSION...

BEGINNING STAGE

*Performed with pressure of **imaginary..or..walking opponent.***

INTERMEDIATE STAGE

*Performed with pressure of **imaginary..or..jogging opponent.***

ADVANCED STAGE

*Performed with pressure of **active opponent...at game speed.***

BENEFICIAL DRIBBLE TRAINING OCCURS ONLY IN AN ENVIRONMENT
THAT FORCES THE PLAYERS TO CONSTANTLY MAKE A DECISION.

FIVE STEPS TOWARD GAINING DRIBBLING CONFIDENCE

Step. 1. **CONTROLLING THE BALL IN GEOMETRICAL FIGURES:**

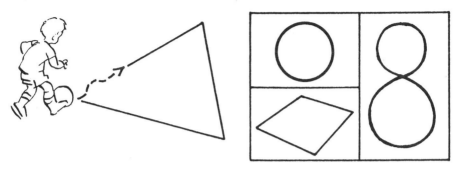

Objective: To touch the ball with every stride or step.

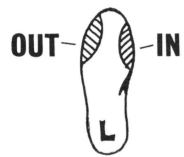 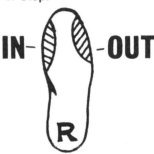

Specific Instructions that can be given:

LEFT FOOT	**RIGHT FOOT**
Outside-Instep (only).	Outside-Instep (only).
Inside-Instep (only).	Inside-Instep (only).
Alternate outside-inside with each touch.	Alternate outside-inside with each touch.
Players choice.	Players choice.

ALTERNATING

• left foot (touch)	• right foot (touch)
• left outside	• right outside
• left inside	• right inside
• left outside	• right inside
• left inside	• right outside

• Players choice — ball touches must be with alternating feet.

WORD OF ADVICE: Decide if player has mastered a working skill level to accomplish these exercises. If not repeat where needed.

Step 2: **CONTROLLING THE BALL IN ZIG-ZAG PATTERNS:**
Encourage touches with the ball on every stride (Rhythm of Tap-Step-tap-Step-tap).

NOTE: Zig-Zag patterns may be marked out or left to the imagi-
nation of the player.

**Zig-Zag Pattern Left Foot-
Two-touch play.**

Sequence: Touch twice outside left,
touch twice inside left.
Continue by repeating.

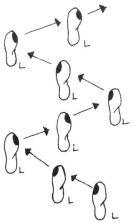

**Zig-Zag Pattern Right Foot-
Two-touch play.**

Sequence: Touch twice outside right,
touch twice inside right.
Continue by repeating.

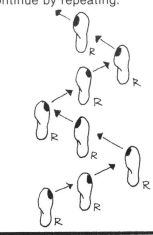

**Zig-Zag Pattern Left Foot-
One-touch play.**

Sequence: Touch once outside left,
touch once inside left.
Continue by repeating.

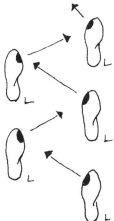

**Zig-Zag Pattern Right Foot-
One-touch play.**

Sequence: Touch once outside right,
touch once inside right.
Continue by repeating.

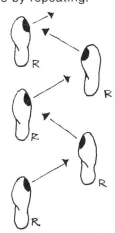

Zig-Zag Pattern Using Both Feet-Two-touch play. (Start Left)

Sequence: Touch twice outside left,
touch twice inside left,
touch twice outside right,
touch twice inside right,
Continue by repeating.

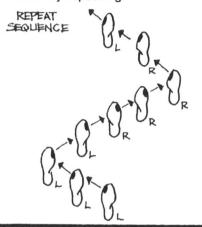

Zig-Zag Pattern Using Both Feet-Two-touch play. (Start Right)

Sequence: Touch twice outside right,
touch twice inside right,
touch twice outside left,
touch twice inside left.
Continue by repeating.

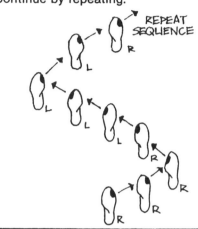

Zig-Zag Pattern Alternating Feet-One-touch play. (Start Left)

Sequence: Touch once outside left,
touch once inside left,
touch once outside right,
touch once inside right,
Continue by repeating.

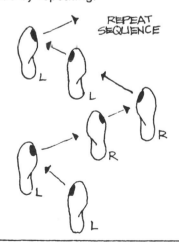

Zig-Zag Pattern Alternating Feet-One-touch play. (Start Right)

Sequence: Touch once outside right,
touch once inside right,
touch once outside left,
touch once inside left.
Continue by repeating.

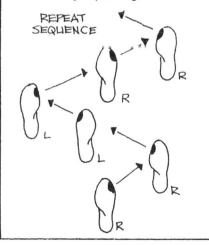

WORD OF ADVICE: It is not recommended to go to step (3) unless a player has mastered these patterns.

Step 3: **FOUR WAYS TO CHANGE DIRECTION:**

A. TOUCH, STOP, STEP and CHANGE DIRECTION.

| TOUCH | STOP | STEP | CHANGE DIRECTION |

B. ROLLING TAP CUT
Touch the ball across the body

| TOUCH | TAP | CHANGE DIRECTION |

C. INSIDE OF INSTEP CUT

Touch the ball across the body with the inside of instep (along big toe).

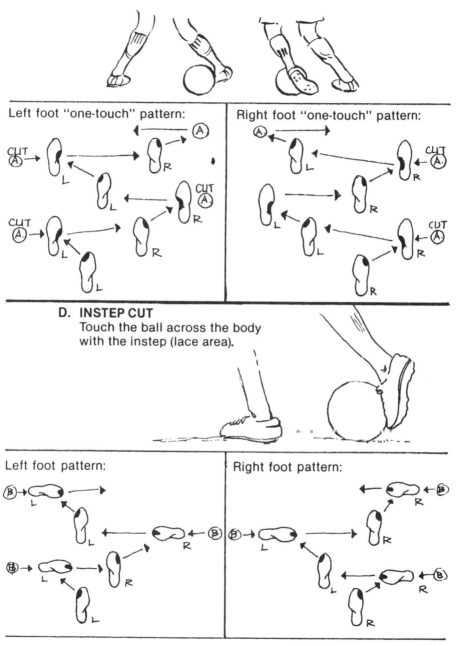

Left foot "one-touch" pattern:

Right foot "one-touch" pattern:

D. INSTEP CUT

Touch the ball across the body with the instep (lace area).

Left foot pattern:

Right foot pattern:

SUGGESTION: Make Step 3: a "Mandatory Exercise for every practice.

Step 4: **ATTACKING FAKES**

All attacking fakes should include the following three requirements:

a. Approach opponent at moderate speed.
b. Give opponent impression that the ball is moving favorably in his direction.
c. Quickly accelerate past the opponent — "Straight Explosion" after fake or feint.

A. SHOULDER FEINT

First movement — Put full body weight on left foot then dip right shoulder. (This will result in opponent thinking attack is to his right).

Second movement — Tap ball with outside of right past the opponent.

B. ONE FOOT OVER

First movement — Pretend to pass the ball with the inside of the right foot but bring the foot over the top of the ball. (This will result in opponent thinking pass is to his right).

Second movement — As foot is returning tap ball with outside of right past the opponent.

64

C. ONE FOOT OVER — OTHER FOOT TAP

First movement — Bring left foot over the ball and plant to the left side and ahead of ball. (This will move opponent to his right).

Second movement — Tap ball with outside right past the opponent.

D . ONE FOOT AROUND — OTHER FOOT TAP

First movement — Bring left foot around the ball and plant to the left side and ahead of ball.

Second movement — Tap ball with outside right past the opponent.

Important: Practice these movements in both left and right directions.

Step 5: **SOCCER TURNS AND FAKES**

> **Important:** While practicing these moves keep in mind that the body is to stay between the opponent and the ball (shielding).

A. STOP AND EXPLODE

First movement — Straight line dribble — moderate speed. On signal slap sole on ball and halt.

Second movement — Read the field to determine where free space exists then "explode" into that direction.

B. STOP — PULL and HALF-TURN

First movement — Stop as above.

Second movement — Pull ball back with sole and make half turn away from the opponent.

C. STOP — PULL and FULL TURN

First movement — Same as A & B except on point of impact of sole on ball then immediately pull ball backwards — 180 degrees — that is, from front to rear.

Second movement — Then reverse body position and go in opposite direction 180 degrees.

D. LOCOMOTIVE

First movement — Pull foot immediately back from ball then "explode" past the opponent.

Note: This fake should momentarily freeze opponent to think a "soccer turn" (See: Stop — Pull and Full Turn) is to result from the move.

E. HOOK-TURN

First movement — Straight line dribble — moderate speed. On signal hook instep around the ball.

Second movement — Swivel on bottom of left foot to move in opposite direction.

F. FAKE-HOOK-TURN

First movement — Same as above except — DO NOT TOUCH THE BALL.

Second movement — Pull foot immediately back from ball then "explode" past the opponent.

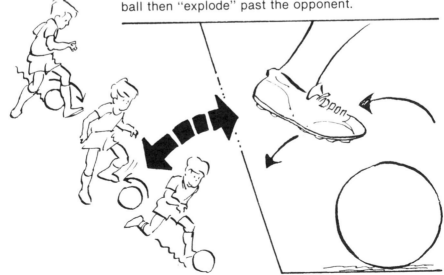

G. STOP · STEP · TURN.

First movement- . Straight line dribble–moderate speed. On signal slap sole on ball and halt.

Second movement- **The same foot** steps over the ball and body swivels in 180 degree direction.

Third movement- Play ball with opposite foot.

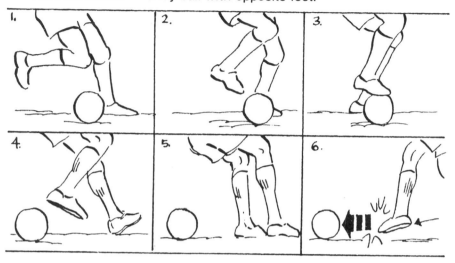

H. FAKE · STOP · STEP · TURN.

First movement- Same as G.

Second movement- Same as G except **do not swivel** in 180 direction.

Third movement- The opposite foot moves behind to tap ball forward.

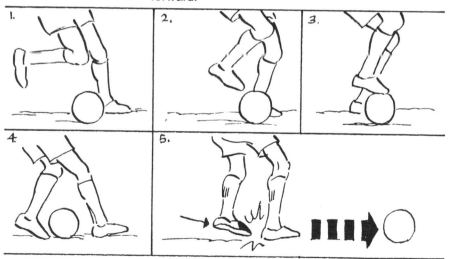

IMPORTANT: Practice these movements in both left and right directions.

SMALL SIDED DRIBBLING GAMES

RULES:

1. Teams should be of even numbers:
   Examples: 1 vs. 1
              2 vs. 2
              3 vs. 3
              etc....

2. Each player has a specific number of touches to make with the ball before release.
   NOTE: The more skilled the player — increase number of touches.
   Infraction of this rule: – loss of ball possession or,
                            – goal for the opponent.

3. Enforce "man to man" marking.
   • one player being responsible to cover a specific player on the opposing team.

4. Encourage a certain fake or feint.
   • give points for beating an opponent with designated move.

5. Scoring goals.
   • touching object - cone or milk carton.
   • putting ball through marked gateway.
   • beating opponent with designated fake or feint.

6. Size the playing area according to the number of players and their skill level.
   • INCREASE size of field — If players are unable to get past their opponent.
   • DECREASE size of field — If players are getting by opponent too easily.

7. Remember: The fewer players per team — the more touches with the ball.

   VERY IMPORTANT: Knowledge is gained by players as a result of following the above rules and guidelines, as opposed to coach verbally reprimanding the players.

DRIBBLING
GAMES TO SEE HOW MUCH PROGRESS HAS BEEN MADE.
CONTROLLED GAME

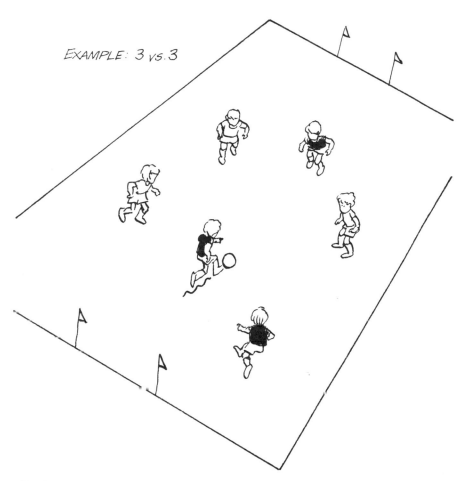

EXAMPLE: 3 vs. 3

- Designate certain fakes and feints to be used in beating the opponent.
- Designate expected number of ball touches per player before release.
- Man to Man coverage.

FREE GAME: Controlled by the players.
- Discipline yourself to know when to leave the players alone.
- Over-coaching can often do more harm than no coaching at all.

THEME
THE USE OF THE INSTEP FOR SHOOTING

Scoring goals is what the game of soccer is all about. It is actually FUN to be able to score a goal, if in practice or in the game. The most widely used technique used for this purpose is the instep kick, which consists of:

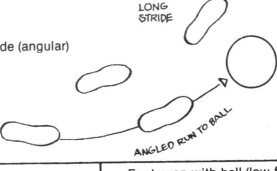

THE APPROACH:
- Slightly from the side (angular)

THE PLANT FOOT: (Non-kicking foot)
- Relaxed monkey stance (knees bent)
- Placement of this foot determines the height and direction of the kicked ball.

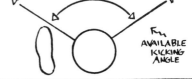

a. Foot even with ball (low flight)

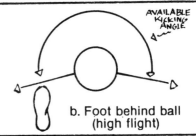

b. Foot behind ball (high flight)

KICKING LEG:
- On backswing, bring heels as close to buttocks as possible. Make toes rigid and lock ankle.
- On forwardswing — keep toes rigid and ankle locked.
  1. Snap knee at contact with ball.
  2. Toes move across body toward the open palm of opposite hand.

CONTACT POINT: Laces of the shoes

72

FUNgames

JUGGLING

Equipment: One ball for every player

Field of Play: Hard surface

Objective: Controlling action of the ball

Steps that should be followed by a beginning player;

1. Hold ball shoulder height, arms extended with elbows locked.
2. Release ball to ground.
3. After bounce on ground have player, using instep, tap ball in air to return to ground. Repeat.

   Sequence: Right Instep — Bounce — left Instep — Bounce

6. Advanced Players: Eliminate ball touching ground.

FUNgames

SOCCER TENNIS

Equipment: One ball for every game.
Field of Play: Hard surface with dividing line (net)
Number of Players: Singles or Doubles.
Objective: Return ball over line (net) on volley or after one bounce.
Rules: • Tennis rules apply.

• Start game by server throwing ball in air to himself.

• After ground contact server then taps ball with foot across "net" (line).

• Opponent may volley or return ball after one bounce on his side.

Winner: First player to reach eleven points.

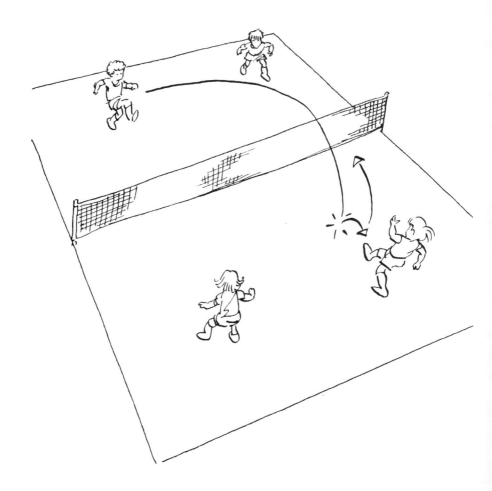

FUNgames

"FOUR CATS"

Equipment: Four balls and four cones

Field of Play: Confined area

Number of Players: No limit

Objective: Get as many "mice" as possible by touching players with
ball below waist

Rules: "Cats", four players with ball, start in their corner
(marked by cone).

- Other players "mice" run inside grid and avoid being touched by ball.
- "Mice" touched below waist by ball go to the corner of the appropriate "Cat".

Winner: Last "mouse" to get caught.

"Cat with the most "mice" at his cone at the end of the game.

CAT & MOUSE (Dodge Ball)

Equipment: One soccer ball per player
Field of Play: Outlined area with two safe-lines
No. of Players: No limit.
Objective: Not to get touched by the ball below the waist.
Rules: • One player "CAT" has a ball — all other players MICE start without ball.
  • On signal from "CAT" the mice run to get by cat and over safety line.
  • "CAT" kicks ball at mice and attempts to hit them below the waist.
  • Once mouse is hit, he also becomes a "CAT".

Winner: Last player to get hit by the ball below the waist

VARIATION: CAT & MICE (Dodge Ball)

Equipment: One soccer ball per player.
  One "BIG" marker.
Field of Play: One line and marker.
No. of Players: No limit.
Objective: Not to get touched by the ball below the waist.
Rules: • One player "CAT" starts the game with ball.
  • On Signal from "CAT" the mice run around the marker and back.
  • "CAT" kicks ball at mice and attempts to hit them below the waist.
  • Mice that get hit by the ball (below waist) become "CATS".

Winner: Last player to get hit by the ball below the waist.

76

One player — One ball

ROLL AROUND
While seated, using the hands to roll the ball around the body and outstretched legs.

BICYCLE
While seated, move legs in a pedaling motion, passing ball under alternate raised leg.

STOMACH ROLL
Roll the ball under the hips and over the stomach while in a prone position.

SIDE TO SIDE
Clamp ball between ankles — lay flat on the ground with legs raised high (knees locked). Touch the ground with ankles on right and left side of body.

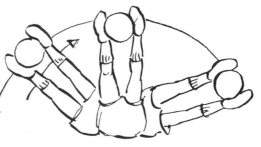

TESTING-INSTEP KICK

Objective:

1. To establish the players proficiency in performing the Instep Kick.
2. To develop a training session so that players are challenged to go beyond their present skill level.

Example:

You observed a problem in accuracy over 15 yards.

Theme: Improvement of kicking over 15 yard distance.

Suggested Test:

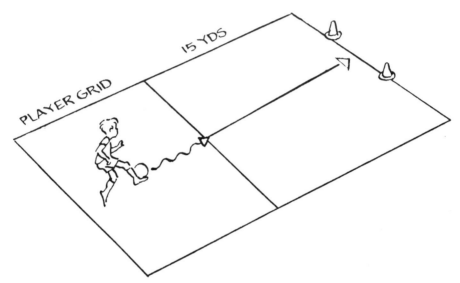

Score card: Out of 10 Attempts

SCORE	CONCLUSION	NEED	ACTION
1-3	very poor	Demo/Explain/Practice	FUNdamental Stage
4-5	weak	Demo/Practice	Game related Stage
6-7	good	Practice	Game condition Stage
8-10	excellent	Play	Small sided game *Special rules— –teams must be even –one touch play

NOTE: Avoid comparing negatively or positively one player against another. Rather, have player be motivated by desire to self-improve.

Instep Testing Continued:

Equipment: One ball for every two players.
Field of Play: • Player Grid — 5-10 yards.
  • Distance grid to target — Vary according to player's ability.
  • Goal Size — Vary according to player's age.

PLAYERS GRID	DISTANCE GRID	DISTANCE GRID	PLAYER GRID

INCREASING TESTING DIFFICULTY:

1) Dribble ball straight — alternating right and left foot shot.

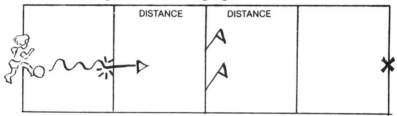

2) Dribble ball across grid — turn 90° for immediate shot.

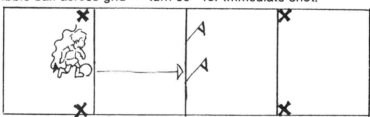

3) Dribble ball away from target — turn 180° (using soccer turn) for immediate shot.

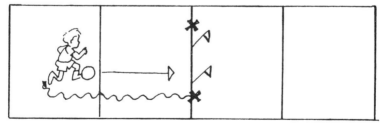

Note:
1. Count number of successful kicks between cones.
2. Player must shoot from inside Player's Grid.
3. "X" marks the spot where player begins action.
4. Based on player's score corrective action should be taken. (See Chart on previous page).

Instep Testing Continued.

1) STRAIGHT SHOT—

Player pushes ball from outside Players Grid using one touch — takes shot with second touch.

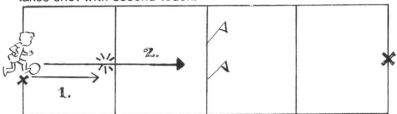

·2) SIDE SHOT—

Player pushes ball across Players Grid using one touch — then takes a shot on goal after making 90° turn.

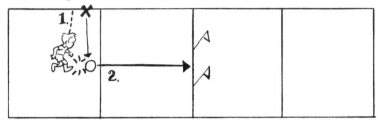

3) REVERSE SHOT—

Player pushes ball away from goal into Player's Grid using one touch — then takes shot on goal after making 180° turn (shot follows turn immediately).

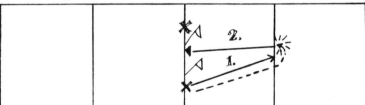

TO INCREASE DIFFICULTY FURTHER:

1) Increase size of the Distance Grid.

2) Decrease size of the goal mouth.

3) Name the number of successful shots expected. (Example: Must make 9 out of 10).

4) Peer pressure (challenge a teammate of equal caliber).

5) Set a time limit.

WORDS OF ADVICE: Do the testing in the prescribed order. Be sure the player is successful on one test before attempting a more difficult level.

NOTE: This testing sequence may also be used for passing.

KEEP SHOOTING PRACTICES REALISTIC

Do not use stationary balls as
part of shooting practice.

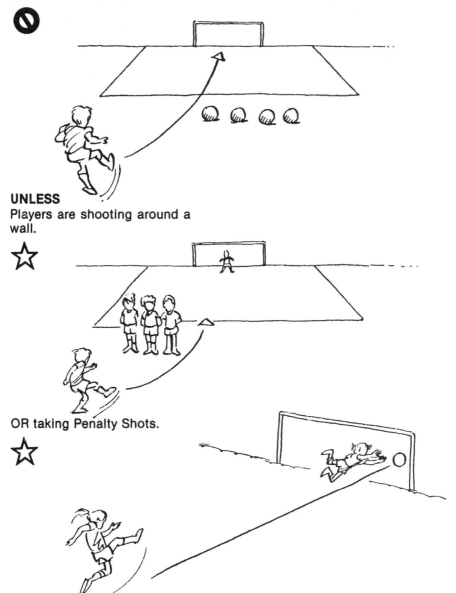

UNLESS
Players are shooting around a
wall.

OR taking Penalty Shots.

IMPORTANT: Shooting practices become beneficial when they resemble
game conditions.

TEACHING CORRECT USE OF INSTEP

1) Against a Wall

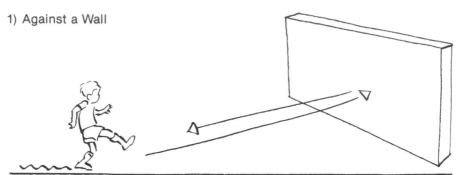

2) Regulation Goal Size <u>with No Goalkeeper</u>

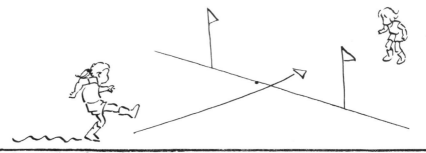

3) Regulation Goal Size <u>with</u> <u>Field Player as Goalkeeper</u>

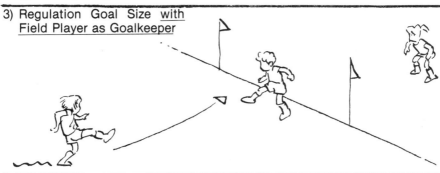

4) Regulation Goal <u>with Goal-keeper</u>

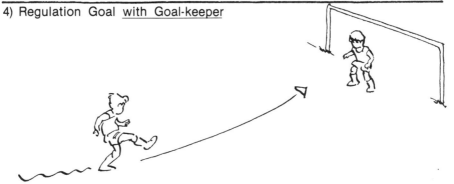

Instep Training (Self serve)

NOTE: Organize all shooting exercises so that some players shag balls.

Goal width — regulation size for that age group.

1. Shoot moving ball

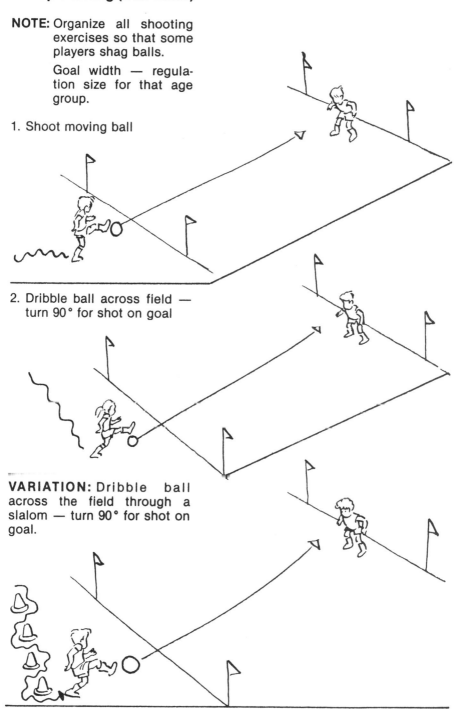

2. Dribble ball across field — turn 90° for shot on goal

VARIATION: Dribble ball across the field through a slalom — turn 90° for shot on goal.

Self Serve (Cont.)

1) Do an exercise (Ex: forward roll or Push-up before taking immediate shot.

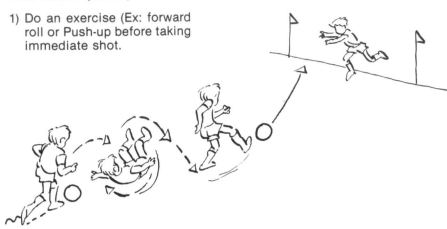

2) Dribble ball away from target — turn 180°. (using soccer turn), then shoot.

VARIATION: Dribble away from target through slalom — turn 180° (using soccer turn), then shoot.

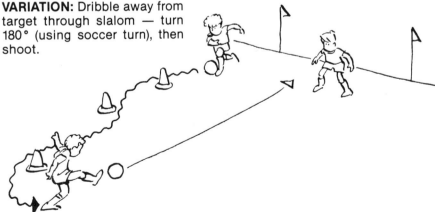

Self Serve (Cont.)

1) Go around an obstacle-take shot immediately.

1-1

2) Jump over obstacle — take shot immediately.

1-1

0) DIRECTION SHOOTING: Coach points which side shot is to be taken.

THEME
HOW TO USE THE INSTEP RESULTING FROM A PARTNER'S PASS.

Only after the player has mastered the art of the instep kick (self serve) should the coach introduce a working partner (partner serve). The level of difficulty to execute each instep kick increases — depending on the point of origin of the pass.

Three types of serves may be given:

1. Through Pass — the least difficult.

SERVED AHEAD

Note: Take a large stride ahead of the ball with plant foot. This allows the ball to roll into a low kick position.

2. The second serve — from backward pass.

SERVED BACKWARD

Note: Make contact through the middle or slightly above the mid-line of the ball — very little follow through.

3. Across the player — the most difficult.

Common requirements to perfect these three kicks:
• Concentrate on accuracy.
• Keep the head down and steady.
• Strike through the middle or top half of the ball.

TESTING
INSTEP KICK IN GAME SITUATION.

Objective:

1. To establish the players level in performing the Instep Kick resulting from partners pass.

2. To develop a training session so that players are challenged to go beyond their present skill level.

Example:

You observed a problem in Instep Kicking a moving ball. Resulting from a through pass.

Theme: Improve the INSTEP KICK when the ball is moving ahead of the player.

Suggested Test:

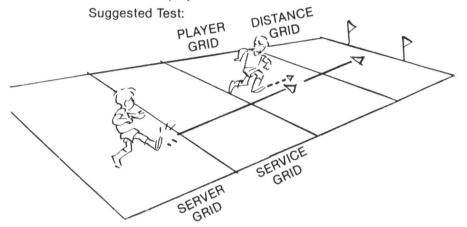

Score card: Out of 10 Attempts

SCORE	CONCLUSION	NEED	ACTION
1-3	very poor	Demo/Explain/Practice	Fundamental Stage
4-5	weak	Demo/Practice	Game related Stage
6-7	good	Practice	Game condition Stage
8-10	excellent	Play	Small sided game *Special rules— –teams must be even –one touch play

NOTE: Avoid comparisons with others. Encourage each player to concentrate on self-improvement rather than on keeping up with others.

Instep Training (from Pass)

REACTION SHOOTING:

Roll the ball between the kicker's spread legs. The kicker "explodes" to take a first time shot on goal.

VARIATIONS:
- Face the server.
- Serve ball left and right.

COME & SHOOT.

Kicker sprints away from goal towards the server then turns onto the ball for a first time shot on goal.

Note: Vary speed and type of serves (Ex: bouncing ball).

Instep Training (Cont.)

DRIBBLE AROUND THE OBJECT:
Step 1. Dribble from the corner of penalty area around object.
Step 2. Pass ball to a receiver.
Step 3. Receiver returns ball first time.
Step 4. Take immediate shot on goal.
Step 5. Start sequence with next ball.

SPRINT AROUND THE OBJECT:
Step 1. Sprint from the penalty spot around an object to receive a pass from a server.
Step 2. Take immediate shot on goal.
Step 3. Continue sequence.

VARIATION: Increase the distance of object from Penalty spot and/or server.

Instep Training (Cont.)
AROUND THE SERVER:
Step 1. The kicker sprints around each server.

Step 2. Each server who kicker has gone around passes ball into penalty area.

Step 3. Kicker takes immediate shot on goal.

Step 4. Continue sequence by going around next server.

VARIATIONS: • Increase distance of servers from goal
- Timed event with points for goals scored
- Contest among players

PRESSURE SHOOTING:
Step 1. Kicker stands inside Penalty area and shoots each ball released by servers (first time).

Step 2. Server passes next ball at the moment ball has crossed goal line.

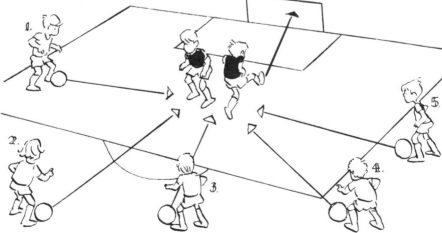

VARIATIONS: • Serve ball in rotation.
- Serve ball at random.

Instep Training (Cont.)

NUMBERS SHOOTING
(One vs. One)
Step 1. Split group into two equal teams.
Step 2. Give correspondent number to each pair of players.
Step 3. Coach calls a number and passes the ball into play.
Step 4. Players whose number was called challenge for the ball and a shot on goal.

Note: Keep score.

NUMBERS SHOOTING
(Small Sided Game)
Step 1 and 2. Same as above.
Step 3. Coach calls two or more numbers—these become teammates and challenge same numbers from opposing team.

Note: Keep score.

VARIATIONS:
- **Move groups farther away from the ball.**
- **Player must do exercise before challenging for ball (Ex: push-up).**

SMALL SIDED GAMES INSTEP KICK.

RULES:
1. Teams of even numbers:
   Examples: 1 vs. 1
   2 vs. 2
   3 vs. 3
   etc....

2. **ATTACKING TEAM** is limited to ONE-touch play once inside "shooting range".
   Example: Coach marks out where shooting must begin—

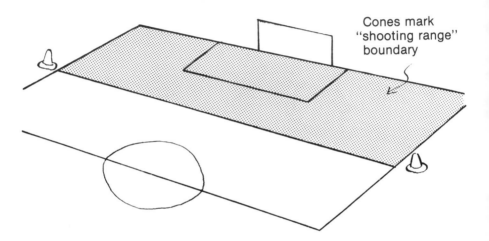

Cones mark "shooting range" boundary

• Coach can call out for certain individual to take shot.

   INFRACTION: • loss of ball possession or
   • point for the opponent.

3. **FIELD SIZE**
   • If very few shots are being taken—decrease the size of the playing area.
   • If shots are not challenging to player—then increase size of playing area.

4. **SHOOTING RANGE AREA**
   • If very few scores are occurring—mark shooting range closer to the goals.
   • If scoring comes too easily—then move shooting range further out.

5. **NUMBER OF PLAYERS**
   Fewer players involved allow for increased number of shots on goal.

KEY: Confidence in shooting will be achieved when player is consistent in accuracy and purpose.

GAMES TO SEE HOW MUCH PROGRESS HAS BEEN MADE.

CONTROLLED GAME. Altering the game in such a way that a particular technique or tactic is emphasized.

Example: **PENALTY AREA GAME.**
Equipment: One ball — One Goal.
Field of Play: Confined area in front of goal.
Number of Players: 1 vs 1 up to 3 vs 3.
Objective: Score goals.
Rules: • Neutral goalkeeper puts ball in play with high toss.
• One-touch play for both teams..
• Shot must be attempted with every ball touch.
Winners: Team with most points at time limit.

FREE GAME: Controlled by the players.
• Discipline yourself to know when to leave the players alone.
• Over-coaching can often do more harm than no coaching at all.

NOTE: This game allows the players time to practice what they have learned and the coach to critique his teaching.

COOL DOWN:

Many coaches fail to remember the tremendous physical/mental punishment their players must endure during practice and game situations. The cool-down period must become an integral part of every coach's training/playing routine.

THEME:GROUND PASS

Children are naturally going to "hog" the ball. This is good for the beginning player. Only after the player has gained basic skill and self-confidence should he then be introduced to "team and teamwork".

Team and teamwork begin with:
    1. Instep pass (laces) — to partner

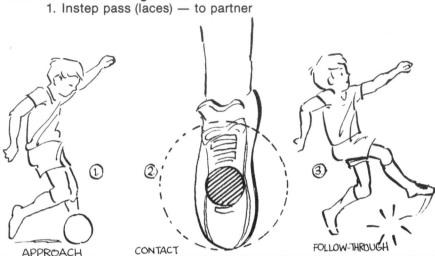

2. Instep pass (outside)

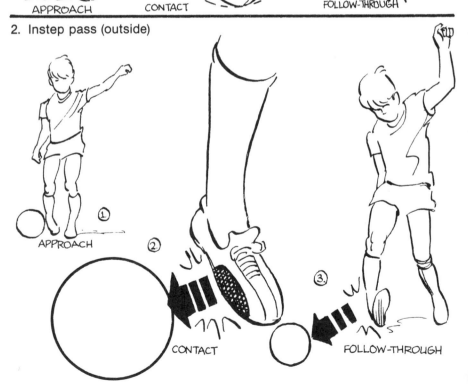

3. Instep pass (inside) – to partner.

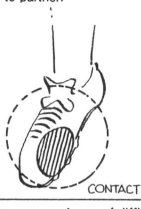

| APPROACH | CONTACT | FOLLOW-THROUGH |

Advantages of using these types of passes:
- easy to disguise intent.
- can be executed without breaking running stride.
- can be used over long and short distances.

Areas of difficulty:
- small area of shoe and ball contact.
- more difficult to keep under control.

---

4. Push pass (cup of shoe) – to partner.

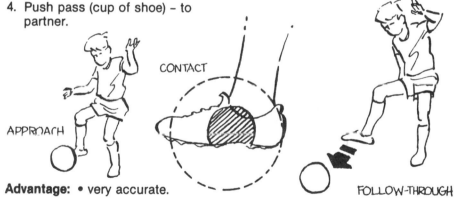

CONTACT

APPROACH

FOLLOW-THROUGH

Advantage: • very accurate.

Disadvantages: • predictable.
- only good over short distances.
- hard to execute when running fast.

KEY: Let them practice what comes natural.

Common to all four passes:
- use relaxed "monkey stance" both knees are slightly bent throughout the passing movement.
- begin each pass by bringing the passing foot behind the plant foot and use a pendulum type swing.
- lock the ankle before contact with the ball.
- Follow through.

95

SOCCER MARBLES.

Number of Players: One vs. one.

Field of Play: Open area.

Objective: To hit opponents ball with your ball.

Rules: • Start game with one player passing his ball in any direction.
- Players alternate attempts to hit partners ball.
- Score Two points for hitting moving ball.
- Score One point for hitting stationary ball.

SOCCER GOLF.

Equipment: Nine targets.
One ball per player.

Objective: Hit each target with minimum number of passes.

TARGET BALL.

Equipment: Special ball as "TARGET".

Objective: To knock "Target" ball across opponents line with passed balls.

Rules: – All passes must originate behind own line.

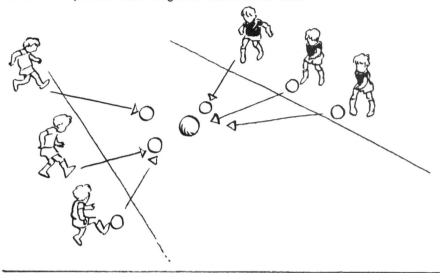

PITCHING SOCCER PENNIES.

Objective: Pass ball so that it stops on target line with one pass.

Rules: – All passes must originate from behind the serving line.

Winner: Player stopping ball closest to target line out of a set number of passes.

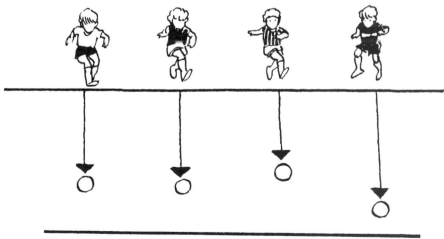

TARGET LINE

SOCCER CROQUET.

Equipment: Objects to make small gateways.
Objective: To get through all gates with least number of touches.
Rules: Croquet.

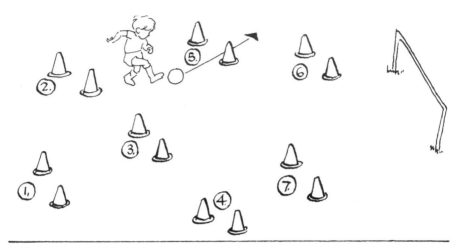

SOCCER BOWLING.

Equipment: Ten objects which can be knocked over by rolling ball.
Objective: To knock over the most pins in ten attempts.
Rules: Bowling.

   Increase distance to pins with better skilled players.

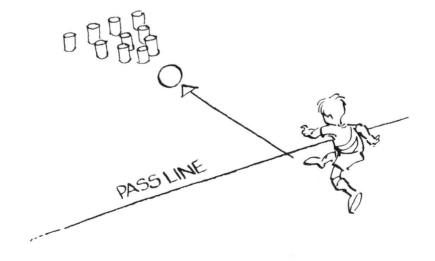

PASSING FUNgames

MOVING GOALS:

Equipment: One or more extra T-shirts.

Number of Players: Two even teams.

Objective: Pass ball under the T-shirt held by two neutral players moving
inside area.

Rules: –Teams interpass while attempting to put ball underneath moving
T-shirt.

FOX HUNT.

Equipment: One colored shirt worn by "FOX".

Number of Players: Two even teams.

Objective: Touch neutral player (FOX) below the waist with ball.

Rule: Rotate players playing FOX every minute.

Winners: –Team with most successful touches.

–Player with least number of touches when FOX.

PIGGY IN THE MIDDLE.

Field of Play: Players standing in a circle – one in center is "PIGGY".

Objective: "PIGGY" tries to gain possession of ball as players move ball one to another.

Rules: – Maximum "two-touch" play.
  – Player from which "PIGGY" gains possession of ball becomes "New PIGGY".

Winner: – Player who never becomes "Piggy" during the game.
  Player who as "Piggy" intercepts most number of passes.

VARIATION: Designate two players to be "PIGGIES".

WALKING SOCCER.

Field of Play: Regulation size.

Number of Players: Two uneven teams.

Objective: Score more goals than the opponent.

Rules: All rules of the game apply – except no one may jog or run(Infraction results in goal for the opponent).

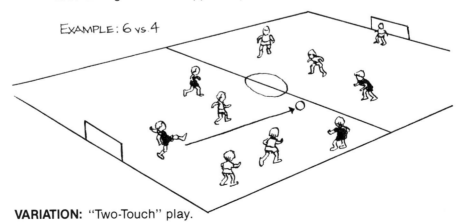

EXAMPLE: 6 vs. 4

VARIATION: "Two-Touch" play.

Two players — One ball

1. Figure Eight — ROLL AROUND

Step 1. While seated, use the hands to roll ball around the body and to the outstretched legs.

Step 2. Leave ball at sole of feet for partner to continue the routine.

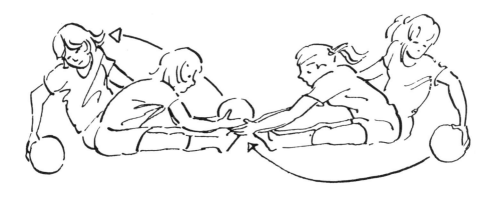

---

2. Step 1. Roll the ball over the stomach and under the hips.

Step 2. Pass ball to partner to continue the routinc.

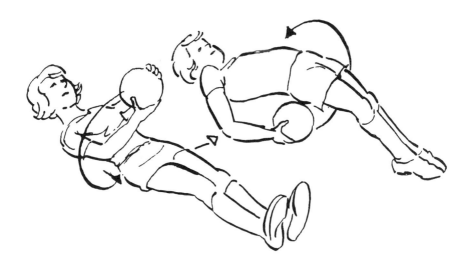

STRETCH
2 Players – 1 Ball

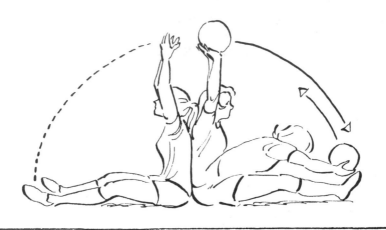

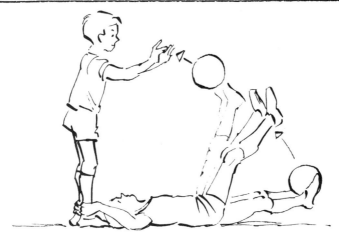

GROUND PASS TRAINING.

1. <u>Passing for accuracy</u> – Pass ball between cones to a partner.

---

2. <u>Pass and Exercise</u> – Give various instructions to be executed after each pass (Ex: push-up).

---

3. <u>Partner Moving</u> – Pass ball to partner and follow your pass then perform an exercise (Ex: leapfrog).

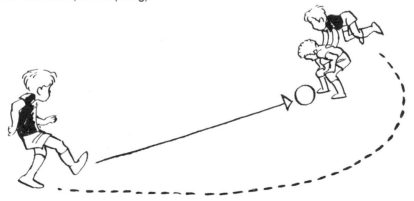

GROUND PASS TRAINING (Cont.)

1. <u>Speed Passing</u> – Count number of passes back and forth during designated time period. (Challenge personal best in future attempts).

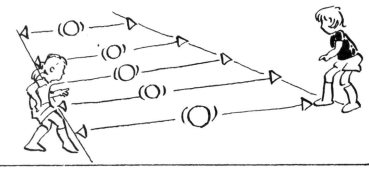

---

2. <u>Accordion Passing</u> – Move further apart after each pass then reverse by moving closer together—

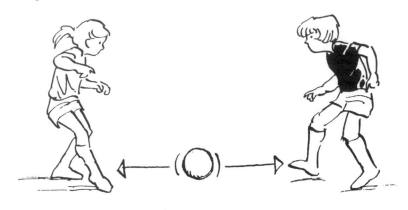

---

3. <u>All Direction Pass</u> – Pass between partners as you jog forward, backward and side to side.

GROUND PASS TRAINING (Cont.)

UNDER THE BRIDGE — Spread legs.
Exercise 1. <u>Stationary</u> - pass ball under "bridge" to partner.

Exercise 2. <u>Movement</u>.
Step 1. Follow pass to become "bridge".

Step 2. Exchange places with player who passed under you - as "bridge".

Repeat sequence in other direction.

GROUND PASS TRAINING (Cont.)

FOLLOW YOUR PASS TO NEW POSITION.
Step 1. Pass ball to partner.

Step 2. Follow your pass to exchange positions.

Step 3. Prepare to receive the pass from third partner.

Step 4. Repeat sequence in other direction.

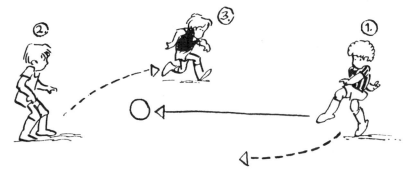

GROUND PASS TRAINING (Cont.)

AROUND THE ENDS.

Step. 1 Start with one worker — and two stationary receivers.

Step 2. Worker passes to 1st receiver and runs around him.

Step 3. Receiver releases ball for worker to pass to next receiver—
continue sequence .

Note: Change worker after one minute.

SMALL SIDED PASSING GAMES.

RULES:

1. NUMBER OF PLAYERS: One team must have at least one more player than the other team.

Examples: 5 vs. 1 beginning players.

           5 vs. 2 good players.

           5 vs. 3 better players.

           5 vs. 4 excellent players.

IMPORTANT: Increase the size of smaller team as skill level in passing advances.

2. SPECIFIC RULES FOR TEAM WITH LARGER NUMBERS.

a. Each member of the team is restricted to "two-touch" play.
  • Ideal "two-touch" play means: Gain control of ball on first touch, then release to partner on second touch.

b. If player touches ball more than "twice" –
  • opponent is given clear possession of ball or
  • opponent is given a goal.

c. Scoring: – putting ball through goal or
  – reaching specific number of consecutive passes without opponent interceptions.
  (Ex: Five consecutive passes = goal)

3. SPECIFIC RULES FOR TEAM WITH SMALLER NUMBERS.

a. Each member of the team is allowed to dribble.
  • Discourage first time kicks.

b. Scoring: – putting ball through goal or
  intercepting passes of the larger team.

4. SIZE of the PLAYING AREA — should be related to skill of players.
  • The higher the skill level the smaller the field.

GROUND PASSING.
GAMES TO SEE HOW MUCH PROGRESS HAS BEEN MADE.
CONTROLLED GAME.

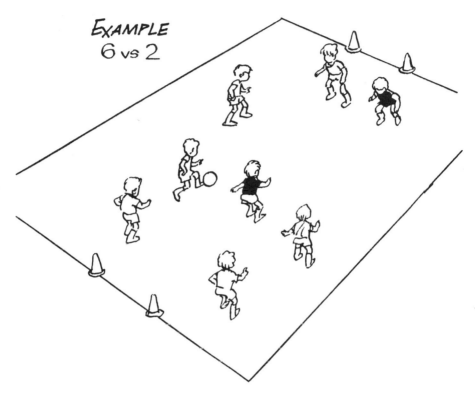

EXAMPLE
6 vs 2

SPECIAL RULES:

6 Players:
- Score between the cones (goal).
- Limited to "TWO-TOUCH" play.

2 Players:
- Score between the cones (goal).
- Score by taking the ball away.

FREE GAME: Controlled by the players.
- Discipline yourself to know when to leave the players alone.
- Over-coaching can often do more harm than no coaching at all.

COOL DOWN:

Many coaches fail to remember the tremendous physical/mental punishment their players must endure during practice and game situations. The cool-down period must become an integral part of every coach's training/playing routine.

THEME: WALL PASS

Ball handling skills should be mastered to a high degree before "combination play" is introduced. "Combination play" means the ability of two players to coordinate body/ball movement in order to get past an opponent. Skilled coaches establish verbal and physical cues for the pattern of play to be attempted.

To execute a proper wall pass the following players are necessary: Player with the ball (dribbler), teammate in proper position (wall), and an opponent (defender).

Step 1. Dribbler moves toward the defender (physical cue).
Step 2. Teammate adjusts right or left of defender
("Reads" — upcoming wall pass).
Step 3. Dribbler passes ball to "wall" who first times ball behind the defender.
Step 4. Dribbler explodes past defender opposite side of "wall" to pick up the through pass.

KEY POINTS:

Dribbler–

–go straight at the defender.
–approach at a controlled pace.
–give a properly paced pass:
    too slow and it may not reach the "wall".
    too fast and it may be deflected out of control.
–explode past defender.

"Wall"–

–sprint into a positive position (facing the dribbler) right or left of the defender.
–give verbal communication (verbal cue).
–approach the ball and give first time return.
–pass (behind defender) in front of teammate.

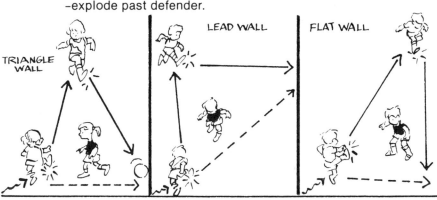

110

TEACHING THE WALL PASS

1. Off regular wall or bench.

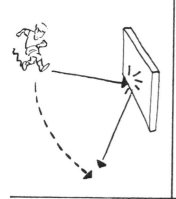

2. Free practice (with a partner).

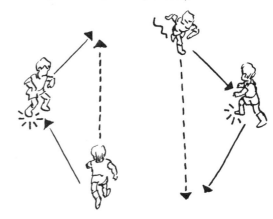

3. Going to an object.

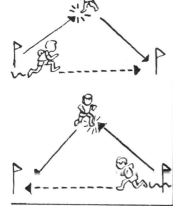

4. Going around an object.

5. Going around a defender.

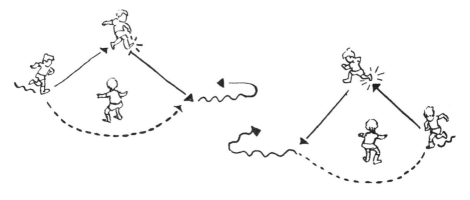

SMALL SIDED GAMES FOR WALL PASS

RULES:

1. Teams of uneven numbers (with a 2 to 1 ratio).
   Examples: 2 vs. 1
              4 vs. 2
              6 vs. 3
              etc....

2. Members of larger team must be allowed to dribble (NO restrictions).
   Reason: The dribbler must go directly at the defender in order to set up a wall pass situation.

   Score goals: As in all other small sided games–except more points are given for a successful wall pass.

3. Smaller team:

   –unlimited number of touches per player (may dribble).
   –discourage first time uncontrolled kicks.

   Score goals:
       –putting ball through designated area or
       –intercept passes from the larger team.

4. Size the playing area according to the success rate of wall passes of the larger team.

   –Unable to get wall passes–increase size of field.
   –Getting by opponent with ease–decrease size of field.

5. Number of field players–depends on success rate of wall passes of the larger team.

   –Unable to get a wall pass–decrease opposition.

   –Getting by opponent with ease–increase opposition.

KEY: Continued repetition of the basics (dribbling & passing) will improve the wall passing function.

112

GAMES TO TEST PROGRESS

CONTROLLED GAME: Altering the game in such a way that a particular technique or tactic is emphasized.

SPECIAL RULES:

3 Players (Attacking)
- Score for successful wall pass
- Score between the cones (below waist).

3 Players (Defending)
- 2 are Keepers.
  1 on Field.
- Score by taking the ball away.

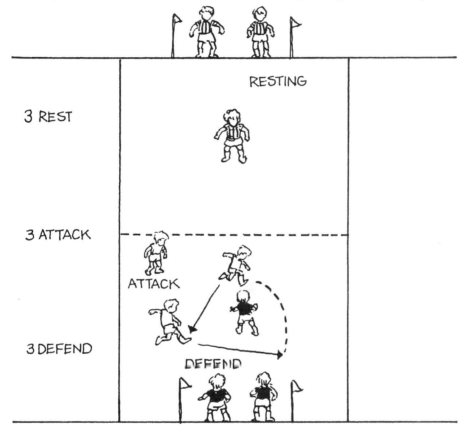

FREE GAME: Controlled by the players.
- Discipline yourself to know when to leave the players alone.
- Over-coaching can often do more harm than no coaching at all.

COOL DOWN:

Many coaches fail to remember the tremendous physical/mental punishment their players must endure during practice and game situations. The cool-down period must become an integral part of every coach's training/playing routine.

THEME
BALL CONTROL: GROUND BALL

The player determines, according to the path of the ball (rolling on ground), which part of the shoe to use for contact (inside or outside). Approaching the ball is of vital importance for two reasons. One, it creates space between oneself and the opponent; two, it helps in bringing the controlling surface into the path of the ball. Timing problems will be avoided by using proper body position and allowing defensive body reactions to carry out the "cushioning" effect.

KEY POINTS:
1. Bring inside or outside of shoe into the path of the ball.
2. Use relaxed "Monkey-Stance" — knees unlocked.
3. Non-receiving foot is aimed toward oncoming ball.
4. Receiving foot is slightly raised off the ground.

Outside — slightly ahead of the plant foot.

Inside — should be totally relaxed-like a "wet noodle"–behind the plant foot.

TEACHING PROGRESSION:
1. Control with one foot — pass with the same foot.
2. Control with one foot — pass with the other foot.

TESTING — CONTROL of GROUND BALL

Objective:
1. To establish the players proficiency in controlling a ground ball.
2. To develop a training session so that players are challenged to go beyond their present skill level.

Example: <u>You observed</u> few players making any attempt to control the ball before passing.

          <u>Theme:</u> Improve confidence in "two-touch" play.

Suggested Test:

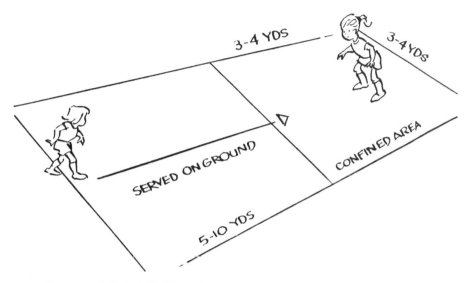

Score card: Out of 10 Attempts

SCORE	CONCLUSION	NEED	ACTION
1-0	very poor	Demo/Explain/Practice	FUNdamental Stage
4-5	weak	Demo/Practice	Game related Stage
6-7	good	Practice	Game condition Stage
8-10	excellent	Play	Small sided game *Special rules— -two touch play -passes must be on the ground

NOTE: Use any game or exercise in this book and apply the "two-touch" rule to that particular exercise or game.

BALL CONTROL: THEME FLIGHTED BALL

When controlling a flighted ball, fear of pain must be taken into consideration. The young player often sees a harmful projectile flying at him, not the soccer ball. The most natural reaction in this situation is to protect oneself or just duck out of the way. Confidence building must be the first procedure in teaching control of flighted balls. The height of the toss can eliminate some of the fears (low at first and increase in height with technique development). The painless and easiest method of controlling air balls is to use the "Metal-Dectector-Trap".

KEY POINTS:

1. Move quickly to bring controlling surface into the flight of the ball.
2. Receiving foot is slightly off the ground (a la "Metal-Detector").
3. "Entire-toe-section" of the shoe is at the anticipated spot where the ball will bounce.
4. Keep the head steady until contact with the "toe-area" is made.
5. IMPERATIVE: DO NOT LET THE BALL BOUNCE.

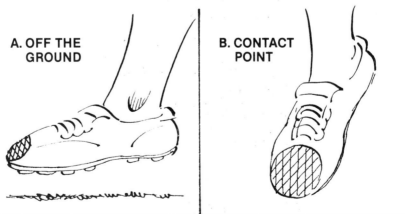

A. OFF THE GROUND

B. CONTACT POINT

TEST — CONTROLLING FLIGHT BALL

Objective:
1. To establish the players proficiency in controlling a flighted ball.
2. To develop a training session so that players are challenged to go beyond their present skill level.

Example: <u>Your observation</u> — few players made any attempt to control a flighted ball.

Theme: Build confidence and improve control of handling flighted balls.

Suggested Test:

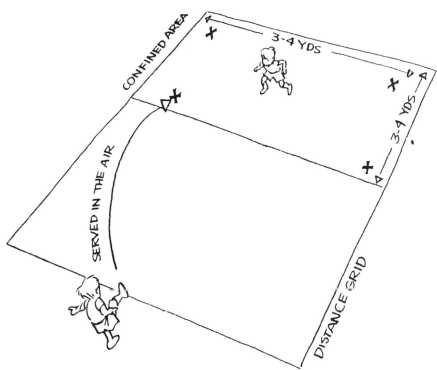

HELPFUL HINTS:

TEACHING AIDS:

1. Begin with low underhand tosses to the shoe area of the player in front of the player.
2. Toss the ball higher as success is shown (but still at the target)
3. Make the player move right and left (give advance notice to side ball will be thrown).
4. Random tosses where the player must adjust the position in order to have a successful control.

THEME
THROW-IN

Laws of the Game — FIFA

LAW XV. — THROW-IN

When the whole of the ball passes over a touch-line, either on the ground or in the air, it shall be thrown in from the point where it crossed the line, in any direction, by a player of the team opposite to that of the player who last touched it. The thrower at the moment of delivering the ball must face the field of play and part of each foot shall be either on the touch-line or on the ground outside the touch-line. The thrower shall use both hands and shall deliver the ball from behind and over his head. The ball shall be in play immediately it enters the field of play, but the thrower shall not again play the ball until it has been touched or played by another player. A goal shall not be scored direct from a throw-in.

KEY POINTS:
1. Part of each foot has to touch ground prior to release of the ball.
2. The ball delivery must originate from behind the head and be thrown over it.
3. The ball must be thrown, not dropped.
4. Both hands must be used simultaneously or with equal force.
5. The player must face the direction of the throw.

TESTING — THROW-IN

Objective:
1. To establish the players proficiency in performing a throw-in.
2. To develop a training session so that players are challenged to go beyond their present skill level.

Example: <u>You observed</u> that most players had difficulty in executing a proper throw-in.

    <u>Theme:</u> To Improve the throw-in technique.

Suggested Test:

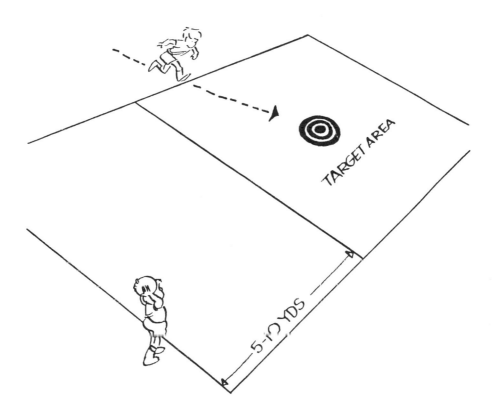

TEACHING AIDS

1. Almost all passing games and exercises can be adapted to teach THROW-IN.
2. Do not start by asking for distance, rather ask for good technique and accuracy.
3. A wall can be very helpful in this practice — allowing for chances at many repetitions.
4. Upper body strength (which is not found in the young player) must be developed before successful THROW-INs can' be expected.

THEME: SMALL SIDED GAMES.

These "games" are governed by rules/regulations that force the player to focus on improving a particular technique while under pressure of an opponent. The competitive atmosphere of the games exposes the player to actual game situations, improves physical fitness and adds the variety needed to prevent boredom.

SOME RULES/REGULATIONS FOR SMALL SIDED GAMES:

1. Beginning players use larger field.
   Advanced players use smaller field.

2. To develop dribbling – use even teams (ex: 1v1; 3v3 etc.) – demands decision making.
   To develop shooting – use even teams (ex: 3v3; 4v4 etc.) – demands decision making.
   To develop passing – use uneven teams (ex: 3v1; 4v2 etc.) – provides needed repetition.

3. To improve shooting – "ONE" touch inside shooting range.
   To improve passing – "TWO" touch play by players on larger team.
   To improve dribbling – "FOUR" touch play is minimum.

4. Use weaker foot for stated period of time.

5. Dribble, shoot or pass using a specific part of the shoe.

6. Keep ball on ground for period of time (below waist line; head etc.).

7. Team may not shoot until all members have touched the ball.

8. Team may not score until all members are over the half-way line of the field.

9. Players may not talk.

IMPORTANT: Be creative – utilize rules that create an atmosphere where the player may work on his particular weakness.

GOAL MOUTH SIZES FOR SMALL SIDED GAMES.

1. Size goal mouth – according to age.
    a. U-6 and U-8 = 6 ft. high and 6 yds. wide.
    b. U-10 and U-12 = 7 ft. high and 7 yds. wide.
    c. All older age groups = Regulation: 8 ft. high and 8 yds. wide.

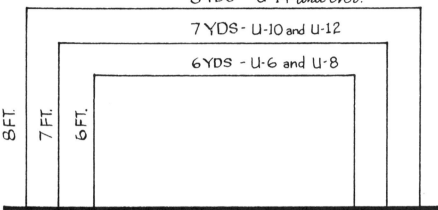

8 YDS - U-14 and over.

7 YDS - U-10 and U-12

6 YDS - U-6 and U-8

8 FT.   7 FT.   6 FT.

2. Small goals – size according to players ability to reach – "playing distance".

| Step 1. Hold cones in hands with feet together. | Step 2. Step as far right as possible (playing distance). Place cone. |
| Step 3. Step as far left as possible (playing distance). Place cone. | Step 4. Result: Ideal small goal size. |

NO GOAL GAME (Dribbling)

Number of Players: One vs. one.
Objective: Maintain ball possession for one full minute (inside grid).
Rules: Player loses ball possession by going out of grid boundaries.

Winner: Player able to maintain ball possession the longest.

NO GOAL GAME (Passing)

Number of Players: Team with large number vs. smaller.

Objective: Larger team wins by reaching a set number of passes to score a goal – say four.

Smaller team wins by forcing ball outside of area OR by touching the ball.

Winner: Team able to reach their objective more often during time limit.

Small Sided Games.

AREA GOAL (Dribbling).

Field of Play: Open space with marked out circles.
Number of Players: One vs. One.
Objective: Bring ball to complete stop inside marked area.
Rule: Ball possession changes hands on foul and after a goal.

Winner: Player with most successful stoppages in time limit.

AREA GOAL (Passing).

Number of Players: Team with larger numbers vs. smaller.

Rules: Players may not stand inside marked circles.

Scoring:
    –Larger team—stopping ball in area (1 point).
        or reaching set number of passes (2 points).

    –Smaller team—stopping ball in area (2 points).
        or intercepting passes (1 point).

SMALL SIDED GAMES USING ONE GOAL:

1. Using any object:

Objective: Attack and Defend the objects.

Words of Advice: Do not allow standing next to objects.

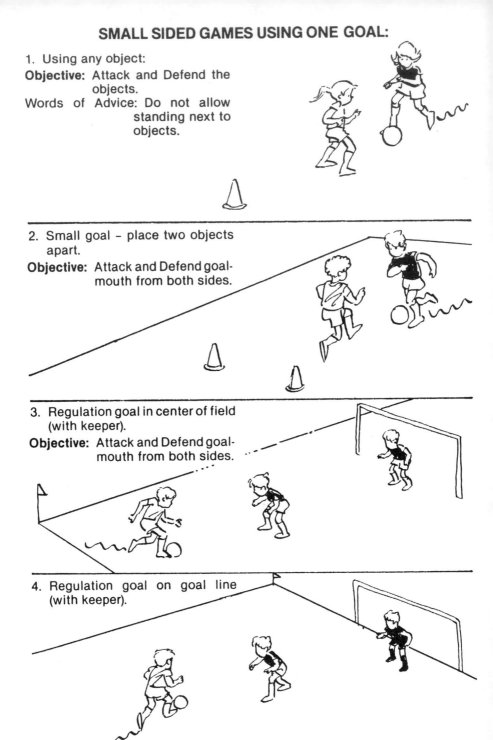

2. Small goal – place two objects apart.

Objective: Attack and Defend goal-mouth from both sides.

3. Regulation goal in center of field (with keeper).

Objective: Attack and Defend goal-mouth from both sides.

4. Regulation goal on goal line (with keeper).

SMALL SIDED GAMES USING TWO GOALS:

1. Two small goals.

2. Paralled goals.

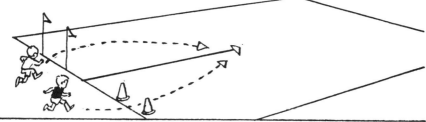

3. Players as goals.

Objective: Attack by passing ball between opponents' spread legs.

Note: Rotate players by calling "switch" every minute.

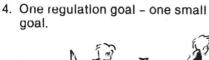

4. One regulation goal – one small goal.

5. Two regulation goals.

SMALL SIDED GAMES USING THREE GOALS:

1. Mid-field goals: Score from any direction.

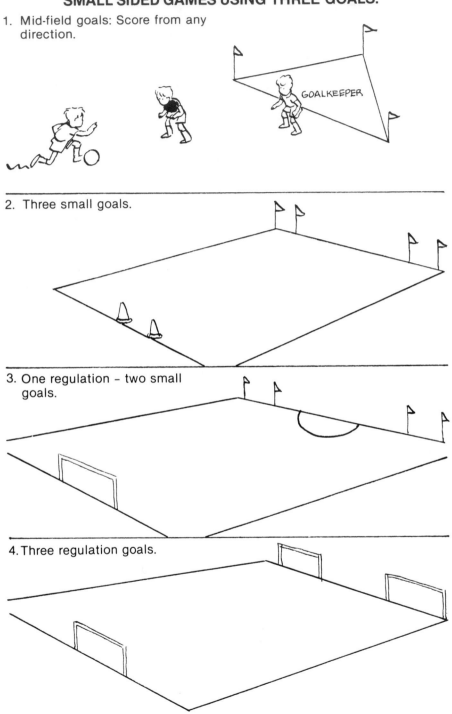

2. Three small goals.

3. One regulation – two small goals.

4. Three regulation goals.

SMALL SIDED GAMES USING FOUR GOALS:

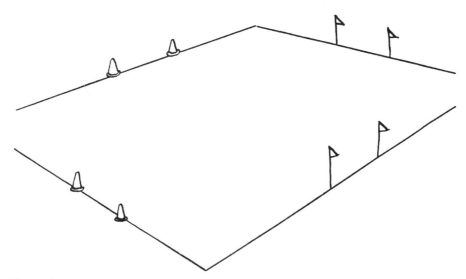

Example: One team Attacks the flag goals and Defends cones.
Opponent Attacks the cone goals and Defends flags.

FIVE OR MORE GOALS:

Objective: A goal is scored when ball goes through goal and is controlled
by a teammate.

SMALL SIDED GAMES (Cont.)
ROTATING ATTACK:

Number of Players: Three equal teams (two neutral keepers).
Field of Play: Full field divided into three parts.
Objective: To score when in ball possession.
To defend after getting a rest.
To rest after ball goes into neutral zone.

Sample Game: Team 1 –defends and tries to get ball into neutral zone.
Team 2 –tries to score and also prevents (1) from getting ball into neutral zone.
Team 3 –is resting until (1) attacks through zone.

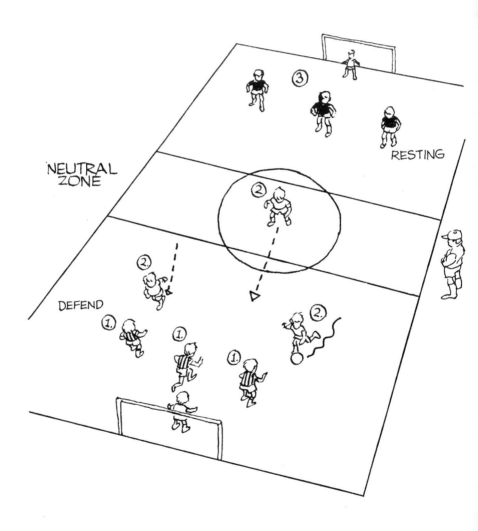

SMALL SIDED GAMES (Cont.)
GOALIE ROTATION:

Number of Players: 4 vs. 4.

Objective: Attack and Defend as a team.

Rules:
- Two players begin game on goal line – two partners in field.
- Play two minutes — keepers and field players change at "switch" call.

Restrictions: Keepers must stay on the goal line and may not use their hands.

Note: Keep accurate time for "switch" call.

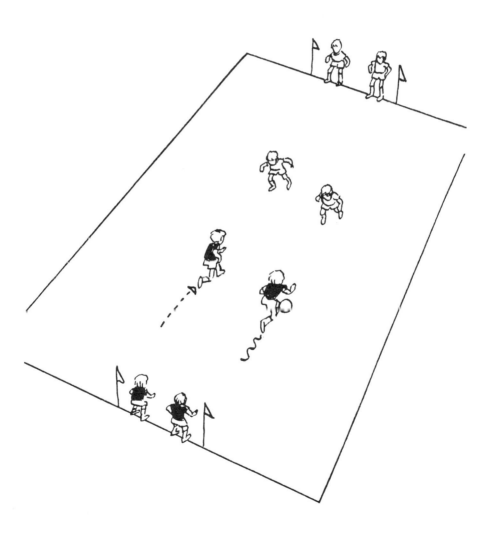

SMALL SIDED GAMES (Cont.)
ALL MUST HUSTLE:

Number of Players: Two equal teams.

Objective: Team can score – only – when all players of that team are across the half-way line.

Note: Stay on half-way line to observe infractions.

NO GOAL

GOAL

IMPORTANT: Be creative – utilize rules that create an atmosphere where the player may work on his particular weakness.

COOL-DOWN
STRETCHING ROUTINE

1) ANKLE: Outline alphabet with the toes.

2) CALVES: In running-start position, lock knee, shift body to lean forward.

3) GROIN: Stand with legs spead, lock one knee, and force that leg inward using body weight.

4) QUADS: Lift leg behind the body, clasp hand around ankle.

5) HAM: Feet about shoulder-width apart and pointed straight ahead. Slowly bend forward until you feel a stretch in the back of the legs. Important: Do not stretch with knees locked.

6) BACK: Indian style sitting try to touch forehead to the toes.

7) STOMACH: In a prone position, plant the heels as close to the buttocks as possible, bring the upper body upward until the back is flat on the ground. Hold to 8 count.

8) NECK: Push head against hand-resistance.

COOL-DOWN: The ruling principle of proper stretching is SLOW & EASY.
The experts WARN against BOUNCING. If a muscle is stretched too fast or too far, the stretch reflex is triggered and microscopic tears occur that shorten the muscle — exactly opposite of what you wish to achieve.